FROM THE CAMPUS TO THE WORLD

STORIES FROM
THE FIRST FIFTY YEARS
OF STUDENT FOREIGN
MISSIONS
FELLOWSHIP

Alice
Poynor

InterVarsity Press
DOWNERS GROVE, ILLINOIS 60515

InterVarsity Press is the book-publishing division of Inter-Varsity Christian Fellowship, a student movement active on campus at hundreds of universities, colleges and schools of nursing. For information about local and regional activities, write IVCF, 233 Langdon St., Madison, WI 53703.

Distributed in Canada through InterVarsity Press, 860 Denison St., Unit 3, Markham, Ontario L3R 4H1, Canada.

ISBN 0-87784-947-1

Printed in the United States of America

Library of Congress Cataloging in Publication Data

Poynor, Alice, 1941-
  From the campus to the world.

  Bibliography: p.
  1. Student Foreign Missions Fellowship—History.
  2. College students—United States—Religious life.
  3. Missions, American—History—20th century. I. Title.
BV970.S64P69   1986   266'.006'073   86-3024
ISBN 0-87784-947-1 (pbk.)

17	16	15	14	13	12	11	10	9	8	7	6	5	4	3	2	1
99	98	97	96	95	94	93	92	91	90	89	88	87	86			

Foreword

The Student Foreign Missions Fellowship (SFMF) in North America celebrates its 50th anniversary in 1986. The 53 college students who organized SFMF in June 1936 with the assistance of Dr. Robert McQuilkin, founder of Columbia Bible College, never imagined their student organization would help mobilize thousands of missionaries for all parts of the earth. God blessed their vision beyond their wildest expectations. Today SFMF is active in 127 Christian institutions across North America. Whether it be Bible college or institute, Christian liberal arts college or seminary, SFMF students are still promoting the cause of world missions.

In 1945 the Student Foreign Missions Fellowship merged with Inter-Varsity Christian Fellowship (IVCF) and became part of IVCF. Since that time SFMF has concentrated mainly on the campuses of Christian colleges promoting the cause of world missions while IVCF has concentrated on the secular college campuses.

In this book written by Alice Poynor, Overseas Missionary Fellowship missionary to Laos and Indonesia, you will find the lives of former SFMF students portrayed with all the excitement and challenges faced by missionaries of yesteryears and today. She aptly described the SFMF movement when she wrote, "On campus SFMF was more than the initial spark. It was its own fuel to keep the goal of missions clear for students." That's still true! The lives of Will Norton or David Howard among other missionaries will challenge the reader. Today Paul and Alice Poynor work together in the Midwest as the representatives for Overseas Missionary Fellowship.

You will be blessed as you read this book that honors three student generations that produced and sent out a valiant group of missionaries who had their roots grounded in the Student Foreign Missions Fellowship while students. Let's keep our eyes on the Lord Jesus Christ, that great Mobilizer of Missionaries.

John E. Kyle, Director
Student Foreign Missions Fellowship

Preface

It's the biggest enterprise of all time. Never has there been a job so costly in its demands, so widespread in its scope or so revolutionary in its impact as that left to the church by its Founder, Jesus Christ.

Call it what you will—missions, world evangelization, global outreach, fulfilling the Great Commission—it remains the greatest challenge ever given. Faced with it, the grandest megacorporation is impotent.

It can never be done. Never, that is, except by individuals willing to be used by the Holy Spirit for God's purpose. This mission demands men and women with courage to change, to risk, to trust, to be involved in taking the gospel of Christ to every creature. God is looking for men and women he can place all over the globe on assignment for him. Throughout the history of the missionary enterprise those men and women have repeatedly come from the student world.

And there's every reason for that to continue.

Today's students have better education, more resources and greater global awareness than at any time in history. Hence they are more crucial than ever to the completion of the Great Commission.

Inter-Varsity Christian Fellowship knows this.

That's why it encourages response to Christ's command through its missions arm, the Student Foreign Missions Fellowship.

The story of the SFMF in its first half-century is the story of students who took God's assignment seriously and banded together to complete it. Their accomplishments bear telling, for God's glory. But they did not finish the job.

Through the encouragement of SFMF, today's students are carrying on where these left off.

Some day the job *will* be done. The saving message of God's grace *will* go out—God promises that. Yet he gives to this generation the opportunity of involvement in history's most significant enterprise and hearing heaven's most satisfying commendation, "Well done, good and faithful servant."

Chapter 1

FIRE IN A HAYSTACK

*S*amuel Mills *read quietly in a corner. He was expected to* be on his best behavior when Mother had a visitor. The adult conversation in the Connecticut parlor went unnoticed until he heard his name. He closed his book and listened.

"I have dedicated this child to the service of God as a missionary," his mother said, smiling across the room at him.

Dedicated . . . to God as a missionary. The idea stuck in his mind. He thought of it as he went to bed that night; he remembered it in the days ahead. In fact, Samuel Mills never forgot that statement. All his life was influenced by the knowledge that he had been given to God for the special task of missions. Missions became his goal, his driving ambition, his life. Even as a teenager his future plans centered not in Connecticut but in the huge, lost world outside America.

Mills went on to Williams College, in Massachusetts. His commitment to God's work grew even stronger. Every Wednesday and Saturday found him alone or with friends in prayer. One favorite spot for their intercession was beside the Hoosack River.

One day under overcast skies they were returning from their prayer spot when the rumble of thunder warned them of an imminent storm. Just as the clouds burst in torrents of rain, they dived for shelter in the only suitable thing that they could see— a haystack. There they huddled, held hostage by the elements. Mills and his friends gave the enforced time to prayer and renewed their commitment to see the gospel of Jesus Christ spread to the world. "We can do this if we will" became their watchword.

Out of that now-famous "Haystack Prayer Meeting" of 1806 came the genetic material that was to form the seed of the Student Volunteer Movement for Foreign Missions. It was the microscopic beginning of gigantic things.

It is here that the story of the Student Foreign Missions Fellowship begins, for it too traces its ancestry from this haystack commitment. But there were intermediate links in the developmental chain.

In 1809 Samuel Mills went to Yale to spread his vision there. What he was urging seems all the more outstanding when we remember that at that time not one American missionary had ever been sent with the gospel to another part of the world. Americans, after all, were still busy conquering their vast, new land. The missionary frontier began at the Mississippi River, not the other side of the world. Nevertheless, Mills and four other students petitioned the Board of Congregational Churches to form an American Board of Foreign Missions for the purpose of sending out four willing graduates of Andover Seminary. As a result of this request by students, the board was formed, and in 1812 the first American missionaries sailed: Adoniram Judson and his wife, Ann, and Samuel Newell and his new wife, Harriet, headed for India. It is a matter of interest that Ann and Harriet's commissioning on February 5 of that year concluded with the singing of the first missionary hymn composed in America, "Go ye heralds of salvation, Go and preach in heathen lands." Six days later, Samuel Nott, Gordon Hall and Luther Rice followed, hoping to join forces with William Carey. But Mills, whose vision spawned the event, was not with them. The board had other plans for him.

They wanted him to spread his zeal among churches in the homeland, urging them not only to support those who had gone but to encourage others to follow. Mills was also sent to investigate the needs among Native Americans. One of these callings would have been enough for most men. But Mills was insatiable in his thirst for challenge. Besides a mission to the Sandwich Islands, Mills led in the formation of the United Foreign Missions Society and the American Bible Society. He wanted to evangelize the slaves whom he saw working around him and formed the American Colonization Society, with the purpose of freeing some, sending them back to Africa with the gospel. Thus the colony of Liberia came into being.

But Samuel Mills had done his work. While returning to the United States from Liberia in 1818, he died at sea. The visionary for what would eventually be the Student Volunteer Movement, instigator of the American mission board, evangelist, organizer and missionary was thirty-five.

His accomplishments in such a few years highlighted the potential of *young* men. And young men responded. First they formed the Society for Missionary Inquiry on the Andover campus. The Young Men's Christian Association (YMCA) followed some thirty years later in 1844. Before long it became concerned with the needs of young people overseas as well as in the United States. Its campus director, Luther Wishard, was so concerned to carry on the original spirit of the Haystack Prayer Meeting that he traveled to Williamstown, Massachusetts, and renewed his commitment at the monument erected on that historic site. In 1883, volunteers at Princeton University joined in a Foreign

Missionary Society, asking for one thousand volunteers for the enormous task of reaching the world.

But it was in 1886 that the next event of real significance to U.S. missions history took place. At the urging of students, Dwight L. Moody led a Bible conference that summer at the beautiful conference grounds at Mount Hermon, Massachusetts. Dr. A. T. Pierson spoke on the theme, "All Should Go and Go to All." At the close of that week, 100 people signed cards indicating their desire to go as missionaries overseas. The plans were laid at that time for a strong, unified movement on the campuses of the nation to enlist students as volunteers for missionary service. The Student Volunteer Movement had been born. The commitment cards for which SVM became known were soon developed.

According to the avowed purposes written at that time, SVM was:

(1) to lead students to a thorough consideration of the claims of foreign missions upon them as a life work.

(2) to foster the purpose of all students who decide to become foreign missionaries, by helping to guide and stimulate them in missionary study and in work for missions until they pass under the immediate direction of the mission boards.

(3) to unite all volunteers in an organized, aggressive movement.

(4) to create and maintain an intelligent, sympathetic, active interest in foreign missions among the students who are to remain on the home field in order that they may back up this great enterprise by their prayers, their gifts and their efforts. It is a recruiting society for the various missionary boards. Its highest ambition is to serve the church.

A grand idea! But would it work?

Within one year, the president of Princeton wrote that he was awestruck "at what this work may grow to. Has any such offering of living young men and women been presented in our age, in our country—in any age, in any country since the Day of Pentecost?" Such was the overwhelming response.

By the time that the first international student missionary convention was held in Cleveland in 1891—five years later—321 individuals had already gone overseas. Over 5,000 more were preparing, and the movement had 6,200 members nationwide.

After two decades, the SVM could report that 2,953 people had gone to the mission field by January 1, 1906. Nearly 150 volunteers a year. That in a day of few academic institutions to draw from and inefficient communications. The SVM seemed to be on its way to fulfilling its motto, "the evangelization of the world in this generation." At the Fifth International Convention of the SVM in Nashville, Dr. George Robson said in his message, "The presentation of Jesus Christ to all mankind is still the supreme business of the church." After 100 years, the flame kindled at the Haystack Prayer Meeting was still burning brightly. And no wonder. It was fueled by the emphasis that the SVM placed on Christian character, development of private devotional life and spirituality. They stressed educating Christians to the needs of the world and encouraging giving for the kingdom. The flame was fanned all across America and on campuses in Canada, Great Britain, Europe and elsewhere. It looked as if the job could be done—the world evangelized in that generation.

On and on until 1920 the fire burned. During that year, nearly 7,000 students attended the SVM convention, and 637 sailed as missionaries. But the cold draft of liberalism in theology and self-centeredness in philosophy made the flame waver. Diverted from its evangelistic task, the SVM began to concentrate on social issues; distracted from its overseas view, the focus shifted to needs at home. Gradually the Student Volunteer Movement flame sputtered. The enthusiasm and numbers of the 1920 convention were never felt again. By 1928, the emphasis was on a search for truth; in 1936, many participants were not committed Christians at all.

In 1934, only 38 students went overseas. In 1940 a mere 465 students attended the quadrennial convention in Toronto. Finally, in 1969, the SVM flame went out completely. The fire that began in a haystack had become ashes.

But one solitary spark kindled earlier in the life of a student volunteer was flickering into a new fire. This time . . . on a mountain.

Chapter 2

A MOUNTAINTOP FOR MISSIONS

*D*own a busy street in Philadelphia walked a determined young minister. New to his church, he was intent on making it grow. He had visited every home on Oxford Street, encouraging church attendance. All at once he caught a movement—a nine-year-old boy darted into a grocery store. The Reverend Anderson followed him.

"Where is the boy that just came in here?" he asked.

The grocer called to a boy, who came out obediently but shyly.

"This is my son, Robert," the man said with a trace of Irish brogue that revealed his origins.

"Robert, where do you go to Sabbath school?" the minister asked. Robert had no answer to that one. So, before long, Robert McQuilkin and the whole McQuilkin family were active participants in North United Presbyterian Church on Master Street.

That may have been the most important visit that the Reverend Anderson ever made. For that little boy was to leave his mark on the Christian scene with indelible strokes.

As he grew older, he was confident of his salvation; his life agreed with his words. After graduation from Central High School with subjects that today would be considered uniersity material, Robert went to work for William Steele and Sons, a Pennsylvania builder. Always a perfectionist, McQuilkin put his all into everything that he did. Now as a Christian he gave his best to his employer, and his efforts were not wasted. Promotions began coming his way.

One evening he walked briskly down the street. Here and there lights snapped on as darkness fell. The breeze was chilly, so he stepped inside the YMCA building. His friends with whom he played handball would be a while yet—might as well wait inside as out. He scanned the bulletin board and then noticed a door open into a class where an elderly man was teaching. McQuilkin walked past the doorway, glancing inside as he passed. Obviously, the lecturer was holding his students' rapt attention. McQuilkin slipped inside. Wouldn't hurt to listen for five minutes or so. He could slip out when his friends came.

What he heard that night was the turning point in his life. The class was on the Bible; the teacher was the Reverend W. J. Erdman, a renowned preacher and teacher and Moody's former pastor. Dr. Erdman's teaching brought him back—regularly for three years!

"Now there's a man who really believes the Bible is the actual Word of God," thought Robert. His heart responded. For the first time he actually heard God speak to him through the Scriptures. It was a thrill that he would not forget, and it influenced his own teaching for the rest of his life.

Business was doing well and his star was rising quickly. He got permission from his employer to work only part-time so that he could go to school. In 1910 he entered the University of Pennsylvania. His mother died shortly after that, and he was released from the financial load of providing for her. Now the challenge of missions began to gnaw at him.

Every year he joined other young people at the New Wilmington Missions Conference, where the emphasis was on taking the gospel to the unreached. But Robert did not feel compelled to head that direction. "God has led me into business," he reasoned, "and by doing it well I can support missions enterprises in a greater measure." There was no indication that he should consider going to the mission field himself. Maybe the ministry eventually, but not the mission field.

The conference did lead him in other ways, though. It was through it that he met his fiancée, Marguerite Lambie, or Margie, as she was called. She encouraged Robert to think about serving the Lord—after all, his zeal and ability were obvious.

The New Wilmington Conference of 1911 was to make a difference. The main speaker that year was Dr. Charles Trumbull, editor of the *Sunday School Times*. His preaching left Robert wanting to know more of the kind of life offered in Christ. He prayed with Dr. Trumbull before that conference was over and came to a new experience of faith in Christ.

It was as if he saw a boat on the ocean of God's grace and he stood with only one foot in the boat, the other on shore. Would he take God at his word and throw himself totally on his grace? He "put both feet in the boat" then and there, and his life became forever after an adventure of faith.

Shortly after this episode, Dr. Trumbull invited Robert to leave his job at Steele's and join him on the staff of the *Sunday School Times*. Robert accepted. He was beginning a new walk with God that would require faith instead of sight, but he knew it was God's direction.

He and Margie were married at this time and her faith reinforced his own. The life of absolute faith—the life lived in victory over sin—that was the kind of life McQuilkin wanted. He was convinced that the preaching of this victorious life was what all

Christians needed to hear. In the fall of 1912, Robert and Margie began a prayer meeting in their home asking God for a Bible conference to be held nearby that would offer the depths of biblical teaching to all who longed for it. The Keswick Conference, which is held annually in Keswick, New Jersey, today is a direct outgrowth of that prayer meeting.

By now McQuilkin was feeling his obligation to a lost world. Together, he and Margie looked for God's guidance concerning missions. They were accepted by the Africa Inland Mission (AIM). Because of Margie's heart condition they could not go immediately, but one year later they were all set.

They were to leave New York on the *City of Lahore* on Saturday, November 30. Trunks packed and preparations complete, Robert went to New York on the twenty-sixth to attend to last-minute customs and immigration necessities. The next morning riding on a city bus he saw a newspaper in a passenger's hand.

The headline said, "*City of Lahore* Sinks in Harbor."

What? The *Lahore*? That was their ship! He had just checked his baggage on her yesterday! This was impossible. But it was true. The ship had caught fire and had been sunk to prevent the fire from spreading to every other ship in port.

But as McQuilkin found out later, their baggage had never been loaded. All their trunks sat on the dock, untouched by the activity—spared from ruin by God's good timing.

For two years, the McQuilkins lived out of suitcases, hoping to sail soon. Finally the AIM advised, "You'd better stay home and take up the conference work that is calling for you." He was in demand for speaking at conferences similar to the Keswick Conference all over the country. Sure now that it was God's leading, he threw himself into conference ministry, preaching what he called "the victorious Christian life."

But the dream of missions that had died that day in New York harbor was to rise as a vision to shape McQuilkin's whole ministry. Within twenty-five years of that event, three hundred missionaries had gone in his place, not only to Africa but to all the world.

Dr. McQuilkin's involvement with missions was just beginning.

The afternoon air shimmered with heat as the ladies gathered one by one. They were not coming for a tea or a game of bridge. That afternoon in South Carolina, a small group of women met to pray.

They were aware of a need for teaching about the deeper spiritual life, about the victory that is ours in Christ. They wanted a Victorious Life Conference to be held in Columbia. And they would invite the man who was the loudest spoken and written voice for the movement, Dr. Charles Trumbull. So they prayed to this end.

But Dr. Trumbull declined their invitation. "However, I can send you someone else for the job," he wrote, "Robert McQuilkin."

So in 1920 began McQuilkin's association with the city that was to become his home. Two years later he accepted the invitation of these same women to head the Bible school that they had shakingly begun on faith. In October 1923, Dean Robert McQuilkin opened Columbia Bible School officially for service to the Christian world. Four regular students and four special students met in two rooms of the Colonia Hotel. This was a venture of faith from the start—the McQuilkins took the appointment with no guaranteed salary but a guaranteed God.

The desire that had spawned the Columbia Bible School also demanded more. There must be a conference in the area where the victorious Christian life could be taught for a week of solid feasting. So the conference at Eliada Homes in Asheville, North Carolina, became the annual event that it is today. Its present site is just around the mountain at the Ben Lippen Conference Center.

Ben Lippen, the "Mountain of Trust," gets its name from the Scottish word *lippen*, meaning "to trust completely, to depend on." A perfect name for a conference that operated completely dependent on God. To the conference center was added Ben Lippen School in 1940. Thus the buildings and land claimed by faith were put to year-round use. School from September to May, conferences from June to August.

It was during this June conference period in 1936 that Dr. McQuilkin felt that the time had come.

One of his frequent warnings to students and others was to point out the syncretism and compromise in the Student Volunteer Movement. Once the great sending force in world missions, the organization seemed determined now to pick out the best in all the world religions and aim at peacefully integrating them with Christianity rather than preach the uniqueness of Christ as the one and only way for all people.

Added to this was another theme that drove McQuilkin to action. He was convinced of the tie between world evangelization and the return of Christ. "The Gospel shall be preached to all nations and then shall the end come," he liked to remind audiences. His biographer states, "This was the driving force in the life of Robert C. McQuilkin. Get the Gospel out to every creature . . . for when this is done, Christ will return."

It was this urgency for spreading the gospel of the kingdom, along with the failure of the SVM to do so that drove him to call for a meeting of students interested in world evangelism, who were willing to take up the failing torch of the SVM for world missions. Over 100 students attended those afternoon sessions at Ben Lippen Conference Center that memorable June. The Student Foreign Missions Fellowship that resulted was a totally student organism. But there is no doubt that it owes its birth to Dr. McQuilkin.

The first local chapter of SFMF, not surprisingly, was at Columbia Bible College, formed at the beginning of the next school term—September 26, 1936—with most of the students as members. From there a team of six men traveled all over the eastern United States, introducing SFMF to other campuses.

"The Student Foreign Missions Fellowship," wrote a Columbia Bible College publication in May 1936, "is a new plan to further missionary vision in colleges and universities throughout the country. . . . McQuilkin spoke of the possibility of this organization giving a new vision to the student world."

It did exactly that. Today there are 127 SFMF chapters on 127 campuses all over the continent. Other accomplishments can be attributed to this great man of faith, but none has had more widespread long-term effects on the kingdom of God than the SFMF.

The men and women whose stories follow are testimony to the vision of Dr. Robert C. McQuilkin and the organization that grew out of it. Take every SFMF chapter across the United States and Canada. Look at all the members of that group who have given themselves to missionary service over its fifty-year history. Multiply that by those won to the Lord in every region on earth through their efforts and attribute it to this: one man who brought the untapped potential and the untouched world together for the kingdom of God.

Chapter 3

A CROOKED FLOOR, A BARGAIN WIFE

Y *ou really ought to go to that conference, Joe," friends*
told him. "Since you've been chairman of the missions committee at Columbia Bible College, missions interest has really
picked up. The missions emphasis at this conference will really
appeal to you."

So Joe McCullough went. It was the first summer conference
at Ben Lippen Christian High School and Conference Center,
in Asheville, North Carolina. Dr. Robert McQuilkin was the
leader. The summer-long chain of conferences has since become
an annual event. But this one in 1936 was different.

Every afternoon, special meetings were held to discuss a new
student missionary organization. The Student Volunteer Movement had lost its zeal and effectiveness. The time had come for
a change and Dr. McQuilkin was the man to lead that innova-
tion. That week the Student Foreign Missions Fellowship was
born. Joe McCullough was elected the secretary.

Joe's own interest in missions was leading him to the summer training program in linguistics sponsored by Wycliffe Bible Translators. So Joe was off to Arkansas when the conference ended. But before the summer was over he was back.

"I want you to return for the final conference and present the new Student Foreign Missions Fellowship," McQuilkin told him. "It's vital that the vision be passed on to other colleges around the country." So Joe returned to give some time sharing the vision for SFMF and its potential to motivate students for world evangelism. Not only at Ben Lippen Conference Center that August, but also as part of a team of six, he traveled around the nation the following autumn.

Tennessee. Chicago. Virginia. North Carolina. Thousands of miles they went, challenging other students with the claims of Christ and urging them to reach out around the world with the message of salvation. Four of the six became a vocal quartet with a repertoire of three pieces. Together in testimony and song they brought the challenge of the unreached world, bouncing from place to place in a Model A Ford.

Though Joe attended Sunday school and church as a boy in Pennsylvania, he did not know what it meant to be a Christian until he was twenty-one. That year, while ushering at an evangelistic campaign at the First Presbyterian Church in Darby, Pennsylvania, he heard a message by Percy Crawford. This and the meaningful music presented by Crawford's male quartet changed Joe's life irrevocably. The following year at Crawford's Pinebrook Bible Conference Joe yielded himself for missionary service. Now he had the opportunity to pass that vision on to others.

But for Joe, missions was more than just a crusade. It was his life. Nothing could hold him from following God's leading to Bolivia. He was sure now that God was directing him to serve with Bolivia Indian Mission, and it was important to be sure it was *God* who was directing him there because there was, by this time, another possible attraction to Bolivia.

Elizabeth Dugan, his fiancée from Charleston, South Carolina, was already there. Her musical and teaching ability, as well as her personal charisma, made her well suited for missionary service. She had gone two years before to teach in a school for missionaries' children. Both of them felt God's real call was to the Quechua Indians, however, and were anxious to begin studying their language. So in October 1937 Joe left to join his bride-to-be.

Bride-to-be in eighteen months, that is. The mission rule required a wait of a year and a half after reaching the field before marriage. It was not eighteen months of idleness. Hard, dawn-to-dusk language study—first Spanish, then Quechua—kept Joe busy. Elizabeth, meanwhile, was studying Quechua in a village hundreds of miles away, thirteen thousand feet up the Andes.

The day came for Joe to move out from under the wing of a senior missionary to study the Quechua language in a country village. He arrived eager for this next step of preparation.

"We have a house for you," the Indians told him proudly. A stone hut about seven feet by fifteen feet clung precariously to a hillside. Through the doorway he could see the corn husks scattered on the dirt floor. Joe ventured a closer look.

No windows, mud roof, obviously a storehouse for fodder. Not only was the house built on the hillside, a commonplace situation, but, Joe realized with dismay, the floor was a hill too. It had never been leveled. Like a magic house of illusions, the floor appeared closer to the ceiling at one end than the other. But this was no trick! It really sloped. Almost eighteen inches. How could you put a bed or table at that angle?

Joe had a problem. After cleaning out the animal food, he set to work. He used the age-old method used by farmers to plant crops on the slopes of a volcano—terraces. One terrace on the bottom for Joe's cot. One terrace on top as a sleeping area for the coworker who soon joined him. And the middle terrace for communal activities such as eating and studying. Each terrace was only six feet square, but it was flat and usable.

Of course, there was no place for a kitchen, so they set that up outside, cooking over a charcoal stove that was bellowed into life each morning and coaxed throughout the day. Cooking was an all-day affair, for at 10,000 feet a chicken was not even chewable until it had boiled for six hours.

But eventually the eighteen-month waiting period was over. Joe and Elizabeth could get married. A civil ceremony legalized the wedding, Bolivian style. Elizabeth, who had been on the field longer, knew better than to pay the first price asked for anything. So when Joe asked the judge how much the wedding cost, the judge answered, "Forty-eight pesos."

Elizabeth stepped in, "Oh, sir, I am not worth that much. Please come down in your price," she told him. But what are a few pesos extra for a good wife?

So Joe paid the full price. "Sure enough, she has proved worth it," he says, laughing.

Now "home" became bigger. A square of four windowless adobe huts arranged with a patio in the middle was their house. "One hut was a bedroom, another the kitchen, the meeting room and a little guest room—all occupied by 'benchucas,' a blood-sucking bug that came out of the ceilings as soon as dark arrived. Added to that, we found after meetings with the Indians, we carried their fleas into our home." To this mansion Joe soon put windows in the kitchen and the bedroom and hung a cheesecloth ceiling to catch the dirt from the roof. Water was provided by the local ditch shared with village women, pigs, sheep, goats and cattle. The outhouse was such a rarity that it proved quite a conversation piece.

But Joe and Elizabeth were there to do a job. And God blessed their efforts. One by one, Indians came to know the Lord and their lives changed. No longer did they attend the pagan festivals of drunkenness and debauchery. Women, too, felt the liberation of the gospel as they huddled around a kerosene lantern, squatting on sheepskins, babies dozing nonchalantly on their backs, listening to Elizabeth teach. The love of the missionaries and the truth of the gospel began to make a difference.

But there was trouble ahead. Satan does not take a challenge lightly. A neighboring town objected to the transformation taking place among the Indians, who one by one were gathered up, marched into town and thrown into prison.

"Stop attending the Christian meetings," they were told. But they refused. So they were beaten. More violence threatened. But still the Indians refused. Joe and Elizabeth dressed their wounds, prayed with them and encouraged them. Some who had been attending meetings were not Christians. Yet they were included in the beatings. Would they disappear under such threats? They did not.

One by one they knelt in the McCullough's adobe living room and received the Savior for whom they had just suffered. The Indians stood firm. Satan was defeated but not finished.

Trouble also came into the missionaries' personal lives about this time. Their first baby died at birth. Grieving, the two young parents renewed their determination. Commitment was commitment. They would go on.

And go on they did, from village to village, walking three or four miles at a time. When they were blessed with a 1930 Model A, they encountered some different problems—mountain roads nearly three miles high, with their killer curves and precipices taking a toll on brakes. "With the car in low gear and both foot and hand brakes on, we often couldn't stop," Joe says. And of course there were always the river crossings, when Indians had to push out the mired Ford and its owners.

Those years have happy memories too, of course. Five boys traveled for a week to attend a week of Bible school one hundred fifty miles away. The joy of learning the Word of God among their own Quechua people beamed on their faces as they stood before a meeting on their return, clean faced and dressed in their best ponchos to sing and tell what they had learned. The joy of seeing transformed lives was a constantly refreshing sight.

After representing the Bolivia Indian Mission in the United States and Canada for a time, the McCulloughs returned to Cochabamba, Bolivia, in 1956. This time Joe was general director.

He traveled. Bolivia, Peru, Argentina, Brazil, Australia, New Zealand, Great Britain. He preached at Bible conferences of his own and other missions. He organized. Citywide evangelistic crusades were held by Bolivia Indian Mission (BIM) in cooperation with other mission groups. Joe was involved in all of this.

During their years in Cochabamba, the first Latin American Evangelical Student Conference was held in BIM's headquarters there. Only ten or twelve young people came, but they represented evangelical students in several countries. At this gathering, they organized and initiated a movement among Christian students that was to continue and bloom till today. In 1958 a magazine was born as the official publication of the International Fellowship of Evangelical Students (IFES) in Latin America. It was called *Certeza*, "the magazine for thinking people." A publishing house called Ediciones Certeza was also founded and is still publishing IFES materials for that part of the world. It was the beginning of a new day for Christian students in Latin America.

The Student Foreign Missions Fellowship had come full circle. Now Latin young people were faced with the same challenge that had brought Joe and Elizabeth from South Carolina to Bolivia thirty years before. Even today, as pastor of a New Jersey church, Joe calls the task of missions "the greatest enterprise in the world—the completion of the Great Commission."

Chapter 4

GETTING THE JOB DONE

*W*ill Norton has a way of getting things done. That might have its origins in his Swedish ancestry. His parents had left their family ties in Sweden to go to the United States. Alone in the city of Chicago they knew only one way to succeed—work.

Mr. Norton worked as a meat cutter, eventually owning his own store. His wife worked beside him in the store and for a time did domestic work in the homes of others to provide for Will and his sister. Those were bleak days financially for everyone.

Mr. Norton, in his eagerness to integrate faith and practice, extended credit to customers who could not pay. As a result, he himself went bankrupt and lost the business.

But if there was a lack of money, there was never a lack of warmth, love and Christian training. Only a block and a half from their home was an Evangelical Free church, whose warm fellowship blanketed Will all his growing-up years. The minister, the Reverend Frank Anderson, was involved in the missions outreach of the denomination, and his concern for the world rubbed off on the round-faced, blond-haired boy.

One negative event punctuated his childhood. At ten years of age, Will became sick. Very sick. "Mastoid infection," the doctor said gravely. "I'm afraid we'll have to operate." Mastoid surgery! The thought stabbed terror into everyone's mind in those days. Medical science was still inadequate to deal with such risk. But the Nortons were driven to increased prayer. The church supported them in it. And Will survived. "God has a special purpose for your life, son," Mrs. Norton said after he recovered. "A very special purpose."

In a boy's memory, though, such dramatic moments are quickly forgotten. Will's energies could have been directed elsewhere. But God had people placed along the way to see that his "special purpose" was carried out. One of those was a faithful Christian leader of the Boys' Loyalty Circle in the church. He was a practical, kind man who loved "his boys." He "modeled the Christian life for me," Will recalls. There were the special meetings, too, held in the First Swedish Methodist Church where the speaker preached on Nicodemus. Will realized that he "must be born again" that night and became a child of God. It took another special series three years later and a dynamic interchurch Crusaders group throughout high school to channel Will's vitality into commitment to Christ.

But did that mean being a missionary? Maybe not. But at a special service at Wheaton College in 1936 Will determined to pray until he found out. Dr. Robert McQuilkin had preached after being ill with pneumonia all week, and, in a marvelous way, revival broke out on that campus. It was an event that had great results in Will Norton's life.

The year of Will's commitment to pray about his service for the Lord was also the year that something had happened on a mountain in North Carolina, which was to play a significant part in Will's life. It was in that summer of 1936 that Dr. McQuilkin led a new movement that grew into SFMF. Will was present at its birth and became one of its early leaders. He enrolled in the graduate school at Columbia Bible College after finishing Wheaton College, and it was there that he and SFMF met.

Will traveled with several of his colleagues as they shared the vision and goals of SFMF on other campuses in the eastern United States. This led later to Will's being elected the second general secretary of SFMF in 1937. Here was a position to develop his leadership ability still further. As general secretary he was responsible for the conference at Keswick, New Jersey, in December and January of 1937-38. It was at that landmark event that the constitution of the Student Foreign Missions Fellowship was accepted. But exciting as the work of SFMF might be, it was not to get in the way of Will's real goal. He was certain now that God was pointing him to Africa.

On the campus at Columbia was a sophomore girl whom Will had occasionally dated. Colene shared his enthusiasm for missions but was not sure that that meant joining forces with this big Swedish graduate student who was pursuing her! Nevertheless, the more they prayed about it, the more convinced they were that they were in love and that it was God's will for them to serve him together in the Belgian Congo under the Evangelical Free Church.

So on June 6, 1939, they were married. In April of the next year, they were on a freighter, loaded with gasoline, plying their way across the Atlantic. Twenty-eight days later they touched African shores and began their way inland to the Ubangi area of the Congo.

What a job they found waiting! Norton was sent out with instructions to establish a Bible school for training pastors and evangelists. The goal was to reach two hundred and twenty-five towns in that corner of the Congo with the gospel. The key was Christian lay evangelists and teachers in each town. But elementary schools were needed to train prospective students before they could enter a Bible school. In addition, the schools' programs had to be coordinated and brought under the care of the church.

To do that, the church had to be organized into districts with supervisors who could oversee the development of schools—and on and on. The job was endless. And if you are to have a school, you need books. Where do you get books? Make them. This too the Nortons undertook. All reading and educational materials had to be made from scratch. And what about the students' living arrangements? They had to supply accommodation for from one hundred to one hundred fifty boys and nearly as many girls.

Now down to the nitty-gritty of building a Bible school. The bricks had to be made by hand and burned to give them strength. The trees had to be cut, barked, sawed and trimmed into the correct number of pieces in each required length.

Of course there was always just living. Repairing the house, growing food, keeping good relationships with everyone on the station, relating to the Belgian colonial government with all its demands and, through it all, not neglecting evangelism. No wonder it took nine years to get the Bible Institute of the Ubangi established.

But Will got it done—all the while learning to function in three foreign languages: French, Lingala and the tribal language, Ngbaka. It was not until several years later that he learned that the tribal language with which he was struggling had three tones. No wonder the word for *snake* and the word for *leopard* seemed to be the same. They differed only in tone. The word for *snake,* a visiting linguist later explained, goes up and the word for *leopard* goes down. Will remembered it this way: a snake rises to strike its prey; a leopard leaps down. Even languages could not deter the Nortons.

By now the Norton family included two little boys—Will, Jr., and Peter. Colene had more than enough to do. In fact, the work looked bigger than the workers one day as they took a little time away from the station for rest. Discouraged and tired, Colene awoke one morning with a prayer in her heart. She wanted a new touch from God that would result in answers to prayer, something that would visibly affect the work that they were called to do. As she prayed, God reminded her of a long-forgotten hymn, "Teach me to pray, Lord: teach me to pray. This is my heart cry day unto day. I long to know thy will and thy way: Teach me to pray, Lord, teach me to pray."

Now where was that hymn? She wanted to find it and read it in its entirety. The missionaries with whom they were staying had a big library. Colene looked there for a book that would contain the whole hymn. But it was not to be found. She went back to the room and sat dejectedly by a little table under the window.

The door opened. In came two-year-old Will. He toddled over to her with an open hymnbook in his hand. "Mommy," he said, handing her the book. There in front of her on the open page were the words, "Teach me to pray, Lord. . . ."

"God began a new thing in my life that day," Colene says now. She began to pray for six new missionaries to share the load. Before the year was over there were five new missionaries already on the field and a sixth awaiting passage in New York.

But the years of action had taken their toll. Returning to the Congo from furlough in 1947 with three little boys—Seth had arrived during furlough—the Nortons plunged again into the mass of work that faced them. Then in 1949 a fourth son was born to them. But their rejoicing was short-lived. Timothy lived only three days. Now grief was added to weariness and frustration. Clearly a vacation was called for, so off they went to a primitive area for a rest. But there Colene succumbed to malaria. The cure for malaria was Atabrine. But the cure itself had side effects and resulted in what was called Atabrine poisoning. Her condition worsened. There was no alternative but to come home for medical care. Ten years after making their way to Africa, they were back in the United States, their missionary careers seemingly ended.

Failure? No indeed. What he had learned during those ten intensive years Norton could now share with younger recruits. So Will went to Trinity Evangelical Seminary to teach missions. He became dean, then president. During his administration, the school moved to the new campus, where today over one thousand future pastors, missionaries and lay workers are trained each year.

After fourteen years there, he went to Wheaton College, where he established the missions department and became dean of the graduate school. By his retirement in 1980, the Wheaton Graduate School had multiplied to four times its original size. In Columbia Bible College, at Trinity Evangelical Divinity School and then at Wheaton College, Will had put his experiences into perspective for others. Now he could pass on the job to younger shoulders.

Not quite. God had yet another chapter of accomplishment to add to Will Norton's life.

It was clear to the Sudan Interior Mission that another seminary was needed in Nigeria. The existing one at Igbaga was not keeping up with the explosive church growth. Of two thousand churches, five hundred had no pastor. So again, ready for retirement, Will was asked to get the job done.

The decision was not easy for Colene. Faced with the possibility of pleasant retirement, close to children and grandchildren, the idea of returning to life in another culture was hard to swallow. "Why now, Lord, after all these years? Haven't we done enough?" she pleaded one night through tears.

God's answer was simple. "Colene, what does it matter if you enjoy your retirement years? What does all this matter in the light of eternity?" Colene surrendered, and God gave her peace about the new venture that confronted them. After a year of attending to details at home while Will went on ahead, Colene joined him in 1981. Together they flew back to the work that he had already begun in Nigeria. It was life without material enhancements, since there was often no water or electricity. Chickens cost ten dollars each and eggs three dollars a dozen. But the blessings of God during those years more than balanced the books.

"What if I had said, 'No, I won't go to Nigeria,' " Colene says now. "I can never say 'no' to Jesus. . . . I can trust him. He will put me in the best place for me."

During the next three years, they established a brand new seminary, which graduated its first class in July 1983. It now boasts three Nigerian Ph.D.'s as administrators, a beautiful six-thousand-volume library and over one hundred students—new workers for the task to which Will and Colene gave themselves nearly fifty years ago.

Retirement? "There is no retirement for the child of God," they say. "We are here for one purpose—to do his will." They are busier than ever now, working alongside others to get the job done.

Chapter 5

DIVIDENDS PAID IN FULL

*I*t *was a sunny, beckoning Saturday morning at Camp* Gorton. The boys scrambled impatiently into groups, at the order of their scoutmaster. As they headed out, Kenneth Hood waved to his friend Harry in the other group. Under the nature instructor, "Prof," Harry's bunch was to explore the gorge.

"Stay together," Prof warned them, "and don't try to climb up the sides of the gorge. It's high, it's steep and it's dangerous. Let's go!"

The boys fell into step. But the rocky sides of the gorge were so tempting. Harry and a few others began to climb.

Just a few steps at first. Then on, up and up. How high could they get? A little further—then Harry's foot slipped. In an instant his crumpled body lay 200 feet below in the rocky streambed, lifeless. When Ken's group returned to camp later that day the air was weighted with the news. Harry was dead.

As a twelve-year-old, Ken was stunned. It couldn't be. It was some kind of joke. But it was true. Prof gave the message at the church service that next day, and somehow he sensed that Ken, baffled and hurting at his friend's death, was ready to talk. Alone on a walk they talked about death, eternity, God's promises.

"Would you like to know the Lord Jesus, Ken?" Prof finally asked. Ken's Christian home and church background had prepared him for this. As the leader suggested, Ken found John 3:16 and read it, putting his name in place of "whosoever."

"For God so loved the world that he gave his only begotten Son that if Kenneth Hood believes on him, he shall not perish, but have everlasting life." It sunk in. This was what he wanted— assurance that he was a child of God. "Lord, I believe you," he prayed, and from that day on Ken knew that he had eternal life.

Ken attended a Bible conference in Montrose, Pennsylvania, in the summer of 1928. Dr. Robert Glover spoke on the topic "Investing Your Life." Kenneth responded to the challenge he heard that night. He would invest his life in something worthwhile. He was fourteen.

From that moment on he never wavered. His destination was the mission field. His next step, preparation. For that he enrolled in Wheaton College, followed by studies at Columbia Bible College Graduate School. It was here that SFMF came into his life. It provided information about world needs and specific missions. It encouraged prayer; it kept the challenge fresh. For Ken, it sharpened the focus on his already considered field, Costa Rica, under the Latin America Mission.

For Ken, as for all those present at the formation of SFMF in Asheville in 1936, the challenge of missions was not to be kept quiet. Missions was on God's heart; it should be on students' hearts.

"I wish we could take some of this to other schools, like Wheaton," Ken said one day.

"Well, why don't we? Let's ask if we can get some time off to do that."

So the proposal became a request to Dr. McQuilkin. Ken and five others were released from a week of classes at Columbia Bible College to travel. From campus to campus they spread the flame. Students for missions. Any school with an interested group of students was invited to form a local SFMF chapter.

Wheaton, Ken's alma mater, was the first stop. The Student Volunteer Movement (SVM) on Wheaton campus was weakened due to the change of focus of the national SVM organization. Consequently, the band of hardy missions volunteers on Wheaton's campus that was meeting independently "was ready for a revival of a national student missionary movement along the lines proposed by Dr. McQuilkin and incorporated in SFMF." A chapter of SFMF was formed at Wheaton on that visit. Wheaton students were prominent in SFMF leadership from that day on.

The 1930 Model A that the team used for travel brought its own stories. Ken and a fellow team member bought the sedan in Philadelphia for seventy-five dollars. Later, Ken bought the car himself for use as the SFMF secretary and later as a pastor. When the time came to go to Costa Rica he sold it—again for seventy-five dollars. Not a bad investment!

Meanwhile, Ken's own commitment to invest his life was still clear in his mind. After two summers spent traveling for SFMF during college, Ken was named national secretary of the organization in September 1939. Presenting the challenge of missions at school after school, giving his own testimony of God's leading and being part of the large end-of-the-year conferences at Keswick were significant in Ken's own life. The influence of those days stayed with him during effective years in Latin America.

There was another influence on Ken's thinking during those days, though. Elizabeth had started Wheaton College with Ken. They both went on to CBC and graduated from there in 1939. After marriage the next year, they were ready for the task that God had assigned to them—teaching in the Latin America Biblical Seminary in Costa Rica.

But those were war years. Students from South America and the Caribbean were unable to travel to Costa Rica because of danger from German U-boats. So the opening of seminary was delayed. Students who were already in Costa Rica along with the teachers were put to good use, however. They were assigned to rural areas to evangelize and to help struggling churches.

In spite of only two months' knowledge of Spanish, Ken and Elizabeth were assigned too. Together with two students they rattled along the railway line toward the Pacific to the primitive village of Orotina.

Housing in the town was cheap enough, three dollars a month. And for that they could watch every soccer game free, since the house faced the town's playing field. But then it was not exactly a real-estate agent's dream, either: no glass in the windows, mud floor, outhouse and plumbing that consisted simply of one tap in the back yard. Around this faucet Ken built a shower stall. If the folding chairs and card table, bed and charcoal stove were stark furnishings, there was one delightful contrast—the radio/record player powered by a three hundred-watt transformer. This was the scene in which Ken and Elizabeth settled down to language study under the spreading lemon tree outside the door.

Before they had studied long, a beggar appeared. "Limosna!" he wailed, holding out a thin brown hand. Eager to share their abundance, Ken picked a bag of lemons *(limones)* and handed it to him. Muttering in contempt, the beggar wandered off. Day after day beggars stopped, and each time they seemed ungrateful for the bag of *limones* given to them. When Ken's Spanish had improved, he learned why. They were calling for alms, not lemons!

But in September the seminary opened and the Hoods could move out of their "won't-last-long-at-this-price-but-needs-a-handyman's-touch" house into a San José apartment. Ken began teaching. Elizabeth took charge of the seminary kitchen and dining room. Planning meals, purchasing supplies and supervising students required as much Spanish as teaching did. One day she asked a student to give her three water glasses. His face instantly clouded and he seemed confused. "Why would he react like that?" Elizabeth wondered. She repeated her order for three *besos.* Then suddenly it dawned on her. Embarrassed, she changed her instructions to *vasos.* She had asked him for "three kisses"!

But language improved and opportunities increased. Teaching and administration filled their lives for over twenty years. Then one day the road took a sharp turn. Pope John XXIII was in power in Rome. He ushered in a new day of tolerance toward Protestant Christians and toward the Bible. For the first time that anyone could remember, Catholics were encouraged to read the Bible for themselves. Neighborhood studies for women, children's Bible clubs, evening classes for couples—the doors flung open. Suddenly the Hoods found their Catholic friends and neighbors willing to study God's Word with them. Spurred by the visit of Dr. Abram Vereide, founder of International Christian Leadership, congressional and political leaders began meeting for prayer at a weekly breakfast in the Supreme Court. Ken was enthusiastic about these gatherings. Here people from the upper echelons of Costa Rican society studied the Bible and prayed together. They even went to Washington, D.C., for the presidential prayer breakfast and seminar in 1962. Ken accompanied them and translated when necessary.

This led to a prayer breakfast for provincial governors in Heredia, the provincial capital. Interest grew among doctors, lawyers, businessmen and government leaders.

The ministry opportunities arising from these contacts kept Ken and Elizabeth busy. Contacts led to friendships. Friendships led to opportunities for influencing Costa Rica's future through the lives of her leaders and thinkers.

In 1972 Ken increased this potential by teaching English literature seminars at the University of Costa Rica. Using his own book, *An Anthology of English Prose*, he led students to think about the philosophy and world views of such authors as C. S. Lewis and John Locke. Personal testimony, discussions, term papers—all made an impact on the students' lives.

One particular friend of the Hoods is a member of the supreme electoral tribunal. "His keen mind and clear thinking backed by strict political neutrality have made him the most valued member of the tribunal. We like to think that by helping him . . . we have had a hand in helping the Costa Rican people to maintain free and clean elections over the past twenty-five years."

Ken's life investment made at fourteen has paid off. One evening in Costa Rica, at the close of a study in Romans, an elderly Supreme Court judge said with obvious joy, "When I stand before God and need someone to introduce me to the Father, Jesus will say, 'Father, I have paid the penalty for him and he has trusted in me!' Then he will take my hand and bring me to God." He understood the concept of Christ as mediator.

Results like these are satisfying. For Kenneth Hood, they represent one dividend of an invested life.

Chapter 6

ONE WOMAN, TWO WORLDS

*Y*ou can hardly imagine a greater contrast. A dirt-floored, grass-roofed adobe hut in the sizzling heat of an African village. A high-rise, fully modern apartment in a smog-filled, traffic-clogged Asian city.

The first, Zaire; the second, Taipei, Taiwan.

Yet Phyllis Taylor has worked in both.

Born in Spartanburg, South Carolina, she became a Christian as a child and knew from the age of thirteen that God wanted her on the mission field. In the Christian and Missionary Alliance church where she grew up, missions was the major emphasis. So it was a natural step from Nyack Missionary Training Institute to Wheaton College for an M.A. in education with a view to using it overseas.

While at Wheaton, Phyllis was a regular in SFMF. The speakers, the fellowship with like-minded students, the challenge of prayer meetings all kept Phyllis reaching toward missions.

"The SFMF kept the . . . fire burning in my heart," she says, looking back. "One does not stand still. He either goes forward or backward. SFMF kept me pressing toward God's goal for my life."

Because of her background, Phyllis felt at home with the Christian and Missionary Alliance Church as a mission board and left under that organization for Belgian Congo, Africa, in 1951. Thus began over fifteen years of effective service in African villages. Using the tribal language, Kikongo, and some French, Phyllis taught, organized and directed local schools. She wrote curricula and teaching materials for children's Bible classes. She was overseer of school-building construction, trained adult Bible teachers and directed Christian-education work in many areas. She also traveled, holding Bible conferences and evangelistic meetings throughout the Alliance territory. Meanwhile, she was translating two books into Kikongo and substitute teaching in the Bible institute. There was plenty to do.

Among the training classes for children's workers was one class of six men and one woman. Phyllis had taught several lessons, demonstrating how to use visual aids, make a lesson plan, select a memory verse and so forth. Now it was time for the students to practice. The men had their turn, doing very well. But the African woman looked very shy. "I'm only a woman," she said.

"What do you think I am?" Phyllis replied. "Come on, get up and do it." Two months later, when the same teachers came back to report on their classes, the woman had led more children to Christ than any of the others!

At another station, however, there were plenty of women trainees in the class. But one of them could not read. "How in the world is she going to review the lessons when she gets home if she can't read? She can never remember all we learn here at one sitting," Phyllis worried. But the woman remembered perfectly. When it came time to report on the classes, her testimony was marvelous. God had used her to lead over fifty boys and girls to salvation in just two months.

There was also opposition, of course. In the Lingkula area, a team had been sent from the Bible school to go door to door inviting people to a large outdoor evangelistic rally that was to be held in a week. But while the Protestant Christians urged people to attend, the priest told them not to. The area was strongly Roman Catholic, so the priest's word held sway.

Nevertheless, a crowd of curious onlookers gathered. As the time arrived for the meeting, the local pastor was nervous. Over two thousand people milled about under the palm-branch roof erected for a meeting place. Restlessly, the pastor looked for the team from the Bible college that was to provide the public-address system and music. The crowd was becoming noisier and more uneasy. He decided to begin the service without a loud-speaker, but the crowd paid little attention. It was a relief when the students and staff arrived, set up the system and began to sing. The choir was well trained and the music quieted the mob. As interest replaced restlessness, Phyllis Taylor presented the story of the life of Christ, using flannel-graph figures and a large board. Attention mounted.

But Satan had yet to begin his tactics.

As the pastor stood to preach, the public-address system failed. Valiantly he shouted his message across the open air to the two thousand listeners. He strained to speak louder. Then, as if on cue, truckloads of people drove by, shouting and jeering, their brass band effectively drowning out all but their taunts. As the din lessened and the preacher renewed his struggle to preach, the wind gathered strength. The palm-branch roof swayed and fell with a crash. People ran in every direction. Chaos ensued. There was no sense going on with a service that had that many distractions.

But God was not to be outdone by his enemy. The service continued and at the close over two hundred men and women flocked to the palm-branch prayer rooms, crying and praying for forgiveness of sins and new life in Christ. One who had been a religion teacher for twenty-three years accepted Christ that day. "It was a day in which God gave great victory," Phyllis says.

After some time back in the United States and Canada, teaching and speaking, Phyllis felt led to a change. She was invited to teach at a Christian college in Taiwan.

From Africa to Asia. From rural village to world-class city. From "walking water" (it came when you walked with it) to running water and other conveniences. From eating out of a tin bowl around an open fire to enjoying lavish buffets at Taiwan's finest restaurant. Instead of being stuck in mud or sand, Phyllis now gets stuck in traffic. After the security and restrictions of a mission board, she now works alone as a "tentmaker," supporting herself by the jobs she does.

One woman—two worlds. How do they compare?

"There are lots of contrasts," Phyllis says. "In Africa, girls didn't go to school; in Taiwan everyone competes violently for education. Taiwan is crowded; Africa was not. In fact, there are over six times as many people in Taipei alone as there were in the whole area of Alliance work in Zaire." The comparative wealth of the two countries is of course obvious. But Phyllis notices other, more sobering contrasts.

"Zaire had its fetishes and witch doctors; Taiwan has its idols and fortune tellers. Africa was more responsive; Taiwan is a much harder field. In the Congo, they accepted Christ by the hundreds; in Taiwan, only by ones or twos and only after much struggle."

Whereas in the Congo Phyllis learned two foreign languages, in Taiwan she uses English. In fact, the greatest part of her work is in teaching English as a second language. This pays enough for her to support herself and also opens unexpected doors of ministry.

Her experience at the Taipei Hilton is an example. Besides

teaching in the Taipei American school, the language center, a Christian college and at a YWCA evening school, she was asked to teach the staff at the hotel.

"A former college student of mine was personnel director at the hotel," Phyllis explains. "She asked me to come and teach English at the Grill, which is the finest restaurant in the hotel." At first Phyllis said no, but at the young woman's insistence she agreed. One Monday she taught the staff at the Grill and was treated to a beverage and some baked goods. This led to teaching there two days a week with a free meal included each time.

"Then they asked me to teach the cashiers," says Phyllis. "So I agreed and it was scheduled for three different days with a meal on each of those days too."

The meals were among the best that Taiwan had to offer. They had a buffet. Sometimes it was international food; sometimes Japanese, Chinese, American or other cuisine. "All wonderful food," Phyllis says, "and I didn't have to spend time shopping, cooking and cleaning up."

The classes were small and effective, and soon Phyllis was teaching the hotel's accountants and telephone operators and eventually was director of the whole English program for the hotel staff of seven hundred. She had seven teachers under her.

"When God called me to be a missionary, I never dreamed that he would be feeding me for three years free of charge at the Hilton Hotel," Phyllis laughs. "Just like our great God!"

With these as with all her classes, Phyllis gives a bilingual Bible to each student (any holiday provides an alibi for gift giving) and has many opportunities to share her faith. She feels perfectly free to evangelize in any way she can. Later in her association with the Hilton, she was asked to be English adviser to the credit manager, who had refused to take the position unless she was given help with English correspondence. Phyllis had taken her and her secretary to Christian women's group luncheons, to hear the *Messiah* and even to church on occasion.

For all these people at the Hilton and the Chinese staff of the American school, Phyllis wrote *The Master,* a book based on John's Gospel that gives clear explanation of the way of salvation through Christ. It was written in English and translated into Chinese. A second book dealing with fear has just been translated and published. "I dedicated it to them and gave each one a copy so that they would be sure to read it," Phyllis says. Some have already indicated that they have done so.

Besides teaching biblical studies and Christian education courses, speaking in churches and working in many capacities at the U.S. Navy chapel in Taipei, Phyllis now works as a secretary at Glory Press, a new Chinese Christian publishing house started by one of her former students.

Looking back on two such opposite types and places of service, what evaluation would she make?

"I can't think of anything I would do differently," Phyllis said. "I'm not sorry I went to the Congo. I'm not sorry I came to Taiwan—in spite of the differences."

People in Africa responded more readily to the gospel. One cannot feel sorry for the Chinese in Taiwan when it comes to material possessions—their standard of living far exceeds that of Africa. "If there is anything that compels love and pity for Taiwan's millions, it's their lost condition. Except for the work of God in their lives, they are tragically and eternally doomed."

That is reason enough to keep Phyllis pushing on with no thought of retirement, using every possible means to bring others to Christ. The contrast between her two careers is nothing compared with the greatest contrast of all—the agony of eternal punishment versus the joys of heaven. She wants to be sure that many on both continents have a chance to face those alternatives and make the right choice.

Chapter 7

SIX MEN IN A MODEL A

So this was South Carolina! Even the speech of the people reflected the languidness of a sizzling August day to the student fresh from western Canada. Arthur Barber was the son of a plumber from London. Along with two sisters and one brother, he grew up in a thoroughly Christian home in Vancouver, aware of his British heritage. Arriving in Columbia on that day, he was even more aware of his new surroundings and of the commitment that had brought him there.

Steeped in biblical teaching and exposed to missions all his life, Arthur had yielded himself to the Lord for missionary service while attending Metropolitan Tabernacle in Vancouver. It was to train for that service that he had come 2,000 miles southeast to Columbia. There at Columbia Bible College under Dr. McQuilkin he knew he would be well prepared.

He was a little less prepared, however, for the culture shock of a Canadian on Southern soil. Once he was introduced to a Bible class as "Arthur Barber from Vancouver, British Columbia, South America." "I admitted to being foreign," Art says. "But not that much!" Another time, a child in Sunday school asked him to speak a little Canadian to them. There was more than international confusion evident in the birthday telegram that he received from his family on his first birthday celebrated at CBC. "To: Arthur E. H. Barber Columbia Barber College, Columbia, S.C. Happy Birthday stop Philippines won two to six stop Love from all at home."

Besides naming the college after Art, "apparently, the Western Union operator was unfamiliar with the quote of Philippians 1:2-6 given by my folks," Art says now. "The score of the 'win' must have been puzzling!"

In spite of that, Arthur pursued a degree in education, certain that he was in the right place. Columbia Bible College was a spawning ground of missions. No one could swim long in its waters without being aware of world needs. It was, Arthur says, "a campus of the committed." Volunteers were encouraged to spread the word among other students. Six men were chosen to travel as a team to plant new SFMF seeds on other campuses. Arthur was among those six. Besides meeting regularly for prayer and sharing their enthusiasm for outreach with churches and youth groups on weekends, these men traveled from Columbia to Bob Jones University in Tennessee, Wheaton College, Moody Bible Institute in Chicago, and colleges in Virginia and North Carolina. They were an impressive combination.

Gordon Houser was Art's "compatible and tolerant" roommate. Versatile and good natured, he was always willing to leave a college art project to help with a plumbing job that Art was stuck with.

There was Joe McCullough, a friend and prayer partner of Art. Joe had a great burden for the lost and a disciplined dedication to reaching them, but he was not without a generous sense of humor.

"The strong, silent type," Ken Hood was in CBC graduate

school when he traveled with the team. He added a touch of dignity and persuasiveness to the presentation.

Bringing with him the energy and physical appearance of his Scandinavian background was Will Norton, another graduate student. "Will was almost daring, with a wholesome blend of humor," Art says. He brought confidence and enthusiasm to the team's ministry.

The one whom Art calls "our source person for color and a real-life dimension to our witness" was Bill Barnett. "British Bill" had grown up in a missionary family in Africa. He knew the field firsthand. This gave him a quiet, dependable confidence that the others respected.

The tallest of the team, Art joined the others as they compacted themselves to fit in the Model A Ford that carried them on their two thousand five hundred-mile mission.

"We left Chicago late one night on a tight schedule," Art recalls. From Moody and Wheaton College they headed south to colleges in Virginia and North Carolina. The highway was unfamiliar. A thickening fog closed in. There was no time to stop for the night or even to slow down—their itinerary was already packed. Praying as they drove, the men felt "led of God to tailgate a large semi-trailer eastbound." His taillights just ahead of them, they pushed on through the foggy night. If only the driver did not suddenly decide to stop! They arrived at their destination safely. "We kept our appointments," Art says, "but not our cool!"

No record was made of the results of that trip. No journal logs the decisions made, lives changed or dedications affirmed. Chapel periods were limited and time precluded any significant follow-up. "I don't think any of us felt that we were crusaders," Arthur says now. "But perhaps we did stimulate some to think of the global dimensions of the gospel. Maybe eternity will reveal that the Spirit of God spoke" in those initial SFMF team meetings of 1936.

Certainly, for the six team members, involvement with the aims and efforts of SFMF added teeth to their own commitment. All six went on to serve overseas and at home faithfully.

For Arthur that meant Asia. And Annie Lee Thompson. Annie graduated from CBC a year ahead of Art. During her days singing in the CBC women's trio, Art could often be seen in the audience. When it came to SFMF, Art found that Annie shared his interest in overseas service. Moreover, they both became increasingly focused on China as the field of service for them. Finally, engaged, they applied to the China Inland Mission. Ann sailed in September 1938, and Arthur followed a month later.

Language study was the immediate assignment. Ann lived in Tsingtao. Arthur joined the "sons of the prophets"—a group of twenty-two men deep in language study at Chefoo, the coastal town used as a boarding school for the missionaries' children as well as a language school for new workers. Ann and Arthur were in the same province, but language study schedules and mission policy kept them apart except for occasional visits. Later, both moved to the Yangtze valley and eventually on to Chekiang province, a coastal region south of Shanghai. They were always in two separate towns; constantly wading deeper into the language and culture of the people around them.

Those were troubled days in China. At war with Japan and occupied in many areas by Japanese troops, the Chinese people were oppressed and subjected to suffering. China's long and glorious history is full of such distress. Her amazing people carry on, Arthur observes, "eating bitterness yet apparently not embittered; steeped in superstition, yet in no way beyond the enlightening of the Holy Spirit; regimented by foes within and without, yet displaying a sacrificial dedication to the Lord Jesus Christ."

Hundreds lived in abandoned theaters and warehouses as refugees. Those less fortunate were left to the cold night elements on the city streets. Trucks picked up their bodies each morning.

In the midst of such conditions, national pastors, Bible sellers and Bible teachers courageously continued their witness. The gospel, like the people, would not be silenced.

Arthur watched all this. The indomitable spirit, the courage, the unquenchable zeal of those who resisted the enemy. He saw, too, the frequent results of such dedication. In Anhwei province, he stood in silence, looking down at the graves of John and Betty Stam. They, like countless of the Chinese whom they had come to reach, paid with their lives for the spread of the gospel. For Arthur, it was a stimulus for renewed commitment to that same Lord who still demanded, "Follow me."

China goes on. The church of Christ continues. The job of reaching China's ever-growing millions is never ending. But health is a fragile thing, a daily gift from God. For Arthur and Annie, work in that land came to a halt in 1940 when doctors advised their return to the States for the sake of Arthur's health. The situation in China worsened and they never re-entered. Just before leaving Shanghai, Arthur was finally able to make Annie Lee Thompson, Annie Barber. Married at last, they returned to the United States to begin a ministry together.

In church after church, on numerous mission agencies, in home and foreign missions, Arthur and Ann still carried the torch so eagerly picked up in SFMF fifty years ago. Today, at seventy-two, Art still ministers frequently throughout the Midwest. Always he encourages financial support of missions and urges young people to become involved as he did in the spread of the gospel around the world.

Art sums it up best: "I remain a grateful servant of a wonderful Lord. I am concerned to be able to say as he did, 'I have finished the work that you gave me to do.' "

Chapter 8

MISSIONS BY MULE

*J*erry *rose and fell with the donkey's slow gait. The cool air* was refreshing, but oxygen was scarce two miles high in the Andes. Breathing could be difficult. It would be several more hours of bouncing like this before he reached the Indian village. It was only a month since he and Janet had arrived in the area, but already requests were pouring in from remote villages for Jerry to come and teach the Word of God. Muleback was not exactly a rapid transit system, but it got him there.

It was an earlier trip that really got him rolling.

Jerry Gerow had gone to Columbia Bible College to prepare to serve the Lord who had changed his life at age seventeen. He had not known just what that might involve, but he was willing to find out. He attended SFMF faithfully, right from the beginning of his first term. After all, it was compulsory—or so he thought. By the time he found out that it was not, he was hooked. The SFMF was opening new doors for him, giving focus to his plans. He would stay in it.

That included singing tenor in the quartet for three summers. Crowded with the rest of the team into a Model A, they traveled across the eastern half of the country, encouraging groups in other schools. Like everything in his SFMF experience, the quartet trip was good training for what was ahead. That experience also meant learning to pray for a wider and wider part of the harvest field and hearing God's messengers from all over the world. Little by little, God was leading him to South America.

"All my real interest in missions, as well as my knowledge of what God was doing in the world, came through SFMF," Jerry says. "God used SFMF, among other things, to help me find my place in his vineyard."

Finding God's place also meant finding the organization with which to work. At the close of seminary, Jerry and his wife, Janet, a registered nurse, applied to a board for work in Bolivia. But there were roadblocks. The board suggested that they work in the United States for a while because travel was still unsettled at the close of World War 2. So the Gerows made use of the delay by working with the Navajo Bible School and Mission in Arizona and later in New Mexico.

A year later, in 1946, they were accepted for service but delayed because of Janet's health. "On a springboard," thinking they were going to South America, they had no home to which they could return. A Baptist pastor with whom Jerry had served previously invited them back to work there. Through that pastor and a missionary speaker, they became involved with the Conservative Baptist Foreign Mission Society (CBFMS).

"The Lord began to indicate a radical change in our thinking," Jerry says now. They applied to CBFMS. This course was confirmed by Janet's immediate improvement and their acceptance in 1947 for work in Argentina. They've never looked back in thirty-four years in that country. They knew that they had followed God's direction and arrived at the spot that he had chosen for them.

That's where the mules came in.

After one term of working on the sugar plantations in the lowlands, Jerry believed that God had called them to move to the far-western corner of northern Argentina to pioneer in an untouched area. On both sides of the Pan-American Highway there were villages where the gospel had never penetrated, where it was believed that no Christian lived. On furlough in 1953 the Gerows told Christian people of their burden for this region and encouraged them to pray specifically that God would open this new area to the gospel.

On October 31, 1954, they arrived in their new mountain home, a little house on a sheep ranch nine thousand feet above sea level. Exhausted, they unpacked only enough to sleep on and went to bed. The next morning, their new job less than twelve hours old, a man appeared at the door.

"You are an answer to my prayers," he told the Gerows. As they sat around together amid packing crates and trunks, the man told his story. He was the representative for the Bible society for northern Argentina. For some time he had come up to that remote canyon to sell Bibles, but with no response. People were just not interested. In fact, they were even hostile. Discouraged, he gave up and went back to concentrate on the rest of the large area for which he was responsible. But just recently, God had told him to return and try again. Somewhat skeptical, he did so. This time the Bibles sold—to the manager of the trading post, the traders, the Indians up in the hills. Incredibly the atmosphere had completely changed. But the Bible salesman could do only so much. His job was to sell. He prayed for someone to come behind him and follow up the work sprouting all around him. The Gerows were the answer to that prayer.

Over and over the scene was repeated: an Indian would trek down from his mountain home, bringing lamb's wool or llama skins to trade. At the trading post he would exchange them for noodles, salt, clothes—and one of those new books. It would tell, so the missionary said, how the world was made, how people came to be, how to live well—surely worth the few pesos that it cost. Tucked in the saddlebags along with other purchases, the Bible was taken to the remotest villages, where it was read and discussed. What was it all about anyway? And who is this white man who sold it? Maybe he could explain it.

So, as Bibles went out, requests came back. Within three months, Jerry had invitations to thirty villages to teach the truth of "God's Book." But every new product is liable to consumer complaints. The "satisfaction guaranteed" did not materialize for one man. Down to the "distributor" he stormed. Jerry had been in his new area less than one week, and it was his second visit to the trading post. In came a big Indian man, chest and shoulder muscles well developed from mountain life. The friendly hubbub of the trading post dissolved in midair as he strode in. Here was trouble!

Finding Gerow, he began, "A little guy sold me this book a while ago." Jerry knew that he was referring to the Bible colporteur who had welcomed him there.

"He said it would transform my life. Well, it hasn't worked!" he shouted. "Now you come out the back here. I want to talk to you." Jerry did not dare refuse.

Quaking, he sat down at the spot where the Indian pointed. The man began his story. Educated, a one-time worker for the postal service, he owned a carpentry shop now and was a leader of his village. But he was an alcoholic. Now his work was shoddy, his wife had gone, his life was a mess. He had read this book and nothing had changed. Did it work or not?

Jerry began to explain. "It's not just reading the book that will transform your life," he told him, "but accepting it and giving your life to the One it teaches about." He went on to present the gospel. That morning the "big Indian" came to Christ.

Immediately his life changed, his language improved, the furniture he made was again of good quality—and his neighbors were astounded. Word got back to his wife, living in another place, and she too wanted to see this unbelievable sight. She rode back to her husband to ask him about it. He invited her to a Bible study held in his house that evening, when the missionary could explain everything. She came.

The next day, into the Gerows' living room she walked. She was ready to accept the Christ who had changed her husband. The train to her home ran only twice a week: she had two hours till the next one would return. Therefore she wasted no time. "I cannot read," she told the Gerows after praying. "I want you to teach me those Bible verses that you read to me. Teach them to me now before the train comes." So in the hour or so that remained, Jerry and Janet taught her verses from God's Word, bit by bit, over and over till she remembered them. As the whistle blew she climbed aboard, still repeating the Scripture that she had learned.

Wherever the Bible went in the hands of its new owners, it paved the way. When Jerry visited and preached, response was swift and eager. People at home were praying; God's Word was working, and Jerry was on the spot to claim results.

In one village after a weekend visit, the whole village decided jointly to believe. They would all become Christians. Not an uncommon situation in societies where important decisions are always group affairs. But Jerry cautioned, "Great. I'm glad you will all believe, but I want to talk to each one individually to counsel him in this new decision."

The leader agreed. "Line up!" he shouted to his people. The line formed—in the adobe chapel, out into the yard, out of the yard to the desert beyond. Half the day they stood, lined up to talk to the missionary about this new step of faith. It was a rare and wonderful sight to a missionary's eyes.

But as Christians sprang up in more and more villages, Jerry was spending so much time in travel that he could not begin to train the new believers as well as respond to invitations to preach. Bouncing along on a mule again, one day he felt the frustration of the situation. Four days to the village, four days back. It was similar to many of his trips. Muleback by day, sleeping bag by night. It was taking up too much of his time when he should be teaching others. Then God gave him an idea. Why not use the travel time to teach the Indian guide with you?

He called to the man guiding the animals, a new believer. "Would you like to learn a Bible verse while we travel?" He said yes, so Jerry recited a verse, the man repeating a line at a time. Before long he knew the whole verse. Now Jerry pressed, "I bet you don't know what this part means. . . ." And so began an explanation. Mile after mile, day after day it continued. Learn a verse, understand it, learn another verse. It was "Muleback Bible School." Every time Jerry went out he took a different Christian with him, training him in the Bible along the way and in practical experience in evangelism when they got there. Word got around. So popular did these training sessions en route become that, on one trip, Jerry had requests from seventeen men to accompany him so that they could learn as they went. Eventually the training was conducted on a weekly basis in several centers as Theological Education by Extension (TEE) for church leaders who would otherwise not be able to get it.

Jerry Gerow still travels, now in the United States speaking at missions conferences, seminars and universities, as special representative of the Conservative Baptist Foreign Mission Society. He has encountered a few potholes in the road since that first quartet tour, some detours, maybe even a wrong turn here and there. But it has been a good trip! He knows now that SFMF is not compulsory. But it sure started him off in the right direction.

Chapter 9

ONE STUDENT
FOR GOD

*N*ew Year's Eve. *All over the nation, people were clus-*
tered together—families, parties, church groups. On the wind-
swept expanses of central Illinois a group had gathered too. David looked down at the faces in front of him. There was nothing
unusual about spending New Year's Eve together. What made
this gathering different was the purpose that drew them together. Young people from universities all across the country had
given up their Christmas vacations for one purpose—to be challenged by the needs of a truth-starved world for the gospel of
Jesus Christ. They were attending the Inter-Varsity Missions
convention held triennially at the University of Illinois at Cham-
paign-Urbana.

Throughout those days they had been searched by the demands of Scripture, goaded to action by missionary statesmen,
had their interest honed and channeled by representatives of
every major evangelical mission agency in the world. Now they

would celebrate together the death of the One who claimed their lives, by partaking of the Lord's Supper. The mass communion service traditionally marks the climax of Urbana conventions. As the service ended, thousands of young people poured out of that assembly—some silent, some filled with jubilant praise, all forever changed. Many of them would go eventually to all corners of the globe with the message of Christ and his plan of redemption.

It was a thrilling moment for David Howard, the administrative maestro who had orchestrated the whole harmonious endeavor. He thought back to the first such convention, held in Toronto in 1946, when he had been one of the students in the crowd. Five hundred seventy-five young people committed to world evangelism had converged on the University of Toronto that icy week to listen to men such as L. E. Maxwell of Prairie Bible Institute and Dr. Robert McQuilkin of Columbia Bible College lead them to give their lives for missions. The decision card that he signed at that time hung over Howard's desk all through college, a spur that kept him moving forward in his commitment to God's worldwide cause.

At the time of the Toronto conference, Dave was a student at Wheaton College. His brother, a member of a Student Foreign Missions Fellowship group in a Canadian college urged him, "Get into SFMF at Wheaton, Dave, whatever you do."

Dave did exactly that. The weekly meetings and prayer for the world's needs, culminated by the Student Foreign Missions Conference in Toronto, profoundly influenced David. His future was to bear the mark of that influence.

Missions was not new to David. He was one of six children in the Howard family in Philadelphia. All six went into the Lord's work in some way, a tribute to the family life. Phil became a missionary to northern Canada; Elisabeth was a missionary with her husband, Jim Elliot, who was later martyred among the Aucas in Ecuador. Another sister, Virginia, also became a missionary; brother Tom, a college professor; and Jim, a pastor. Their father was editor of an evangelical periodical widely read at that time, the *Sunday School Times*. His parents had been missionaries in Belgium, and their love for God's round-the-world work carried over to their home life. Missionaries came and went frequently. The godly life evidenced in his parents was an influence in David's own life. But when he was ten, he realized that being part of that wonderful Christian family was not enough. It was then he was born into God's family.

That was just the beginning. Gradually, David realized that he shared the responsibility for getting the good news of Jesus Christ to the whole world. And the facts convinced him that most of that unreached world was not in America. So David would have to prepare to go to them—just where, he did not know, but he became increasingly convinced that God would lead him to a place of service in another country. Signing the decision card at Toronto in 1946 was one step in clarifying that conviction.

The SFMF group at Wheaton College helped formulate that decision and continually reinforced it. He was treasurer of the campus chapter and elected president of the national organization in 1946. He was the last national president of SFMF because, by then, the group had merged with the larger Inter-Varsity Christian Fellowship as its missions "arm." As national president, David chaired the newly formed Inter-Varsity Missions Committee. And what a committee! It included such statesmen as Dr. Robert McQuilkin, Dr. William Culbertson of Moody Bible Institute, Donald Hoke of Japan Christian College, C. Stacey Woods of Inter-Varsity and other leading lights in missions and Bible circles around the nation. And the chairman of it all was a college sophomore!

Dave pulled out all he ever knew of parliamentary procedure, occasionally confronting even Dr. McQuilkin, "Pardon me, sir, but you are out of order." Working with those men in this capacity was an experience that Dave was to value later.

Another positive influence toward missions during college days was David's best friend, Jim Elliot. Jim encouraged a small group, including Howard, to meet every morning at 6:30 to pray for more missionaries to go from among the Wheaton students. He also organized twenty-four-hour prayer cycles, during which students took fifteen-minute slots around the clock to pray for missions. He also confronted other students personally with the claim of Christ on their lives. Jim Elliot and four others were killed by Auca Indians in Ecuador in 1956. "But in that short life he would leave a mark for eternity on my life and the lives of hundreds of others," David says.

After graduation in 1949, David served for a year as traveling secretary for IVCF/SFMF. Across the United States and Canada, he visited about one hundred twenty campuses. The trip included traveling from Winnipeg to Vancouver in January and February during the coldest winter in Canadian history. Everywhere he spoke, he urged students to get involved in God's worldwide reachout plan as he himself was planning to do.

By the time he graduated from college, Dave realized something about himself. He was in love! The object of his affection was his friend throughout college, his sister's roommate, Phyllis. Not that he hadn't noticed her before—he was attracted to her on first meeting, and they dated off and on. But "I had lots of competition because she was one of the most popular girls on campus," Howard says, "and I didn't get very far ahead of the competition until the end of her senior year." But by graduation in 1949 David knew he was really in love with Phyllis. So in July of 1950 they were married, and Jim Elliot was best man. Today the Howards have four married children.

David and Phyllis were committed to world evangelism. But where? They wrote to one mission board after another. Replies began to drift back. One mission's warm-heartedness and helpfulness stood out. It was to this mission that Dave and his wife applied. They were to serve happily with the Latin America Mission from 1953-1968.

Their first term of service was spent in Costa Rica. Living in an adobe house in a rural village away from the amenities of the capital city let them in for some surprises. Like the cow—in the living room. When their three-year-old called, Phyllis found a nonchalant, if rather confused, cow standing contentedly in their living room. The grass on which the cow had been grazing out in front led right to the front door, and she kept on chewing her way onward until she was right inside. There was other wildlife too, mostly small creatures such as scorpions, toads, bats, opossums, lizards and tarantulas. Later, David was director of the Latin America Biblical Seminary, which allowed them to live under more "normal" conditions in San José.

Then, in 1958, the Howards moved to Colombia. There he was the mission's field director for Colombia and assistant general director responsible for every aspect of the mission: personnel, business matters, church work, school work, medical work and so on. It was a heavy responsibility and required traveling four times a year to Costa Rica to mission headquarters, besides the frequent travel to isolated rural areas in training laypeople. The church in Colombia during those days was under severe persecution. Guiding the national church in all this yet withdrawing mission control from churches that should be maturing on their own was a major part of Howard's ministry.

In 1968 the Howards came home from Latin America. It was not because his interest in missions had waned; nor was his job done. He had simply changed milieu. He was invited to become missions director for Inter-Varsity Christian Fellowship and director of SFMF (now part of IVCF). He served in that post for nearly ten years. It was a job that included responsibility for missions activities on many university campuses. What a time to step onto the American student scene!

"The counterculture movement was at its height," Dave says.

"We were completely unprepared for this type of thing." Riots and upheaval were the order of the day. Even among Inter-Varsity staff, the feeling was, "Why talk about Timbuktu when Harlem and Watts are blowing up in our faces here at home?" The very concept of missions met with negative response.

"My primary emphasis was to try to help students forget their preconceived notions about missions and missionaries and get into what God himself had to say in the Scriptures." What *did* God say about our responsibility to the world? Loud and clear God gave his answer. Students listened. Some of those most violently opposed to missions later became "the best mission-minded staff members that Inter-Varsity had."

But that was only part of the job. David Howard was now responsible for the ever-growing Urbana convention. He remembers Urbana 70 as a "touchy time." "Students were radically activist in their outlook and many—even those who attended Urbana—did not want any talk about missions." Some even threatened to riot or blow up the convention unless the emphasis switched from missions to current issues: Vietnam, poverty, race relations.

The air was electric as Howard brought the keynote address. He compared the present situation with that of the 1920 convention of the Student Volunteer Movement. The challenge was the same. Would they remain true to the responsibility laid down in Scripture to reach the whole world with the message of redemption, or would they too get sidetracked into political and social activities?

God's Word won the day and Inter-Varsity remained true to its course.

In 1973 and 1976, Urbana was positive and progressive. Urbana 73 experienced three "firsts." Two people who served on the program committee gave excellent addresses—the first student-given messages. Elisabeth Elliot, David's sister, spoke on the role of women in world evangelization—the first full-length message by a woman. And an uneducated Colombian believer, whose life in the power of the Holy Spirit had influenced Howard on the field, preached with power on the connection between evangelism and social concern—the first message given by interpretation.

But the telling factor about any gathering is its effect on the lives of the participants. At Urbana it is a tradition to record this response by having people sign a decision card indicating their willingness to commit themselves to world evangelism or at least to pray about such a step. The decision cards during those tumultuous years tell a tale: 8 per cent of those present signed such cards at Urbana 70, 28 per cent signed those cards at Urbana 73 and 50 per cent at Urbana 76.

Clearly God was at work. From the five hundred seventy-five students attending the fledgling effort in Toronto to over seventeen thousand, the convention had grown. From 8 per cent to 50 per cent, the level of commitment had grown.

From eager student participant to director of the whole endeavor, Dave Howard had grown too. He was now influencing the group that had so effectively influenced him. "There have been few experiences in my life that could compare in gratification and fulfillment to that of sitting on the platform of Urbana looking up at seventeen thousand students" and realizing their potential for world evangelism.

Today as director of World Evangelical Fellowship, Howard continues to have a vision for what SFMF can do. He sees enormous potential in Christian students. What God did at Wheaton through Jim Elliot, what he has done through David himself, what he has done through hundreds of students' lives, he can do through any student—any individual who acknowledges Jesus as Lord.

"I am awed," Howard writes about the Urbana conventions, "by what it would mean if each one would truly make Jesus Christ Lord in his or her life." One student with God is enough.

Chapter 10

PREPARED
FOR VICTORY

*A*pply to the Conservative Baptists for missionary service
and you are likely to talk to a man who knows what it's all about,
in more ways than one. Dr. Raymond Buker, Jr., has seen missions from both sides. Born on the mission field, he knows the
life of a missionary's kid (M.K.). As a worker himself, he has
done the job; as college representative, he saw it from a student's
perspective. Ray could not have planned it that way, but God's
pregame coaching was preparing him for it all.

It started before Ray was born. His father, Raymond Buker,
was an athlete. He and his twin brother were to run in the 1920
Olympics. But the trials were on Sunday. As Christians, they
refused to run on the sabbath and of course could not make the
team. But the trials for the next Olympics in 1924 were not on
Sunday. This time Raymond Buker ran. First he became national
champion for the 1,500-meter and the mile. Then to the Olympics in France.

It was the meet that was to become famous in film and story, the same Olympic games in which Eric Liddell honored God and won. Raymond Buker, too, was able to win. All five top contestants in those days received gold medals and Raymond came home with a gold. Like Eric Liddell, Raymond Buker also became a missionary in Asia, working in the mountains of Burma. This man had become a hero, not only to his countrymen, but also to his son. It was his dad who most influenced Ray's life and who led him to Christ when he was eleven. Ray has been running the race himself ever since.

From the time that Ray was nine months old, he lived in what is called the Golden Triangle—the opium pocket of the world. Here in Northern Burma, Laos and Thailand, poppies produce 60-70 per cent of the world's opium. Women went out early in the morning to slit poppy bulbs and drain the white milk. Boiled and concentrated, this was smuggled by mule trains to the eager outside world.

Growing up means going to school. And school for Ray Buker meant leaving home. Three days' trip by car to a boarding school, Ray went from the time he was in second grade. But that was only for elementary school. Starting at the sixth grade, the journey was even longer—two thousand miles away to India.

By 1942 the Japanese had invaded part of China and Burma. Transportation was cut. The economy was a mess. Lives were in danger. For the children of missionaries, it meant that the safety of school in India could only be reached by walking "over the hump," the mountains separating Burma from India. On foot for five weeks, Ray and others slogged their way to the refuge that awaited them across the border. Although one hundred thousand people never made that refuge, God was keeping Ray—training him for a longer race.

While Ray went to school, Mr. and Mrs. Buker stayed behind in Burma hiding in the jungles as best they could. As long as there was work to be done, they would stay. One day at the school, Ray received a message through the secret service: "We have heard that both your parents have been killed."

It was a staggering report to a sixteen-year-old. For two weeks he struggled with the idea. Then a telegram arrived. Ray was to meet his parents at a railroad station! Not dead, but protected.

It was shortly after this that Ray came back to the United States. He was sixteen, and it was the first time that he had seen the United States since he left it at nine months. This was not "home"; it was a strange land. As a junior in high school, he had a lot of adjustments to make. But it was also a time for thinking and evaluation. Ray did, after all, belong to the Lord. Nothing else could overshadow that. He rededicated his life to God and became more convinced from that point on that God's purpose for him was missions.

Living in another culture, speaking another language, seeing God's faithfulness—it all added up to good training for life as a missionary. But there was more preparation needed, of course. Wheaton College and then seminary followed. But Wheaton was more than just academics.

At Wheaton, God brought Raymond face to face with SFMF and Jim Elliot. As prayer-group leader, Ray naturally got to know Jim that well and prayed with him frequently. "Jim was an outstanding SFMF leader, got top grades, and . . . was an excellent athlete, being one of the top wrestlers on the team," Ray says. Those were days of unparalleled excitement about missions on the Wheaton campus. Jim Elliot made it that way. As far as he was concerned, every student was potential missionary material and should be challenged with the claims of Christ. He had an SFMF representative on each floor of each dorm. They were to visit and pray for each student on their floor, impressing them with the need to give God their life. Jim kept track of attendance at SFMF meetings and prayed for the floors that had low attendance. Jim was one of the big influences on Ray's life as a college student. Running with a winner kept Raymond pushing toward the goal that God had for him. "I was a missionary in Pakistan when I received word of his martyrdom at the hands of the Auca Indians," Buker says. "It made a deep impression upon my life."

From college Raymond Buker went on to seminary. During his first summer, he took a temporary pastorate in Eastport, Maine. God was preparing him here too. His cousin was engaged. At his cousin's girlfriend's home one evening, he was met at the door by a visiting friend, Jean McGregor. Thinking Ray was her friend's fiancé (Ray's cousin), she shook hands and commented on his engagement to her friend.

"Oh, no," said Raymond. "You have the wrong man. That's my cousin. I'm not engaged at all." That was to change. As they talked, he found that Jean was in Maine for the summer earning money to put herself through Bible school. She too was intent on serving the Lord. It was a good start. Gradually they became more than friends. Jean and Ray were later married and have raised five children and ministered together on the mission field and at home.

After a year in a Massachusetts pastorate, Ray and Jean headed for the mission field of Pakistan to work with Muslims. Ray was used to the mission field—he grew up with that kind of life. He was used to living in another culture; no problem there. He was brought up in Asia; Pakistan was in Asia. So it should be very little adjustment.

In theory, maybe. In fact, Ray found it a giant leap from the lush tropical vegetation of the Burma-Laos-China triangle to arid Pakistan. Instead of nearly daily rains, they now had rain only once or twice a year. "This section of Pakistan is the hottest place in Asia," Buker says, and it is dusty dry. Not only the land was dry. Hearts were impenetrable too. Where Burma had been responsive to the gospel, the Muslims with whom the Bukers worked were very slow to come to Christ. The work was discouraging. The people are very different from the Burmese or the mountain tribes among whom the Buker family lived. The languages were not related; even the flora and fauna were new. In fact, Ray Buker says, Pakistan is as different from Burma as from America.

Yet there was a sense in which his previous training had prepared him for this new step. He was familiar with life as a "foreigner"—with separation, loneliness, dependence on the God he served. It was all spiritual muscle toning that made him fit for this challenge.

Jean was prepared, too, though she might not have guessed it when they left America. God had given her the gift of befriending people and showing them hospitality. How well this fitted into the Muslim culture of Pakistan. In a land where women were seldom allowed out of their homes, her visits to them were welcome. She was warmly received—a friend who could bring them news of the outside world and one who cared about them. After friendships were made, the women could come to her house, where through her warm hospitality their lives were touched with the gospel.

Not all their years were to be spent in this hard ministry, however. Their third term plunged them into an entirely different work. The Marwaris were a group of twenty-four tribes, each with their own unwritten language, all traditionally Hindu and totally unreached by the gospel.

One day, Damji, the Marwari leader, trudged toward home, his feet arousing puffs of dust with every step. Suddenly he spotted something on the road ahead. It was a leaflet telling about a correspondence course. A course on the holy book called the Bible. Could this be the truth that he had been seeking? Somehow he felt he was about to find his answer. He enrolled in the Bible course. Surely this was truth. God worked to such an extent in his heart that he and six others made a trip to the nearest missionary, seventy miles away. There all six trusted Christ to save them. They were the first believers among the Marwaris. Now they were open, in fact eager, for a missionary to live among them. Raymond and Jean Buker were just the ones.

Now began a fruitful ministry for the Bukers. They learned to live among the Marwaris, "drink their water, eat their food and use their bedding." They saw many come to Christ, even though they suffered as a result. Moreover, the Marwaris witnessed to their Muslim neighbors, who also came to the Lord. Now Raymond says, "we saw more Muslims come to Christ than when we had actually been working directly with Muslims."

In 1969 Ray was to round a bend and start still another lap. In the midst of the student unrest and campus protests, he was asked to work with college students. After fifteen years away from the States, Ray felt that he was too out of touch with the student world for such a task. But again, he found that God had been preparing him for just that assignment. Experience in Eastern religions and the occult was exactly what was needed to tune into the American student mind of that day. In addition, a sixteen-step plan for reaching a new culture now proved invaluable in reaching the counterculture for Christ. The result was a host of students won to the Lord.

From evangelizing students it was a small step to counseling them about careers in missions. So in 1972 Ray took over the responsibility of personnel secretary for the Conservative Baptist Foreign Mission Society and continues in that role today.

Would anyone brought up on the mission field purposely return to it for his own life's work? For Ray it was no different for a former M.K. than for anyone else. "The dedication is not to missions but to Jesus Christ," he says. Would he encourage others to do the same? Absolutely. It could be overseas or at home—you never know what you might end up doing when you follow the Lord.

God shows you the path as you go along. "We cannot plan for the future," Buker says. "Only the Lord knows it and we walk a step with him." In Ray Buker's experience, wherever that step leads, you find God had been training you for it all along.

Chapter 11

A MAN TO STAND IN THE GAP

*G*ordon Houser was to be an architect. Instead, he followed God's blueprint and found himself in situations that he could not have designed.

"I'm a trouble-shooter," says Gordon. "I've always just gone wherever the need was and helped out." Being a gap filler in God's employ has certainly had its surprises—and its rewards.

Growing up in Philadelphia, "the city of churches," it was natural for Gordon to attend church with his Christian parents. When Gordon's older sister read about the Second Coming of Christ in 1 Thessalonians, Gordon knew he was not ready for that big day. But he knew how to get ready. Kneeling by his mother, he invited Christ into his life at the age of seven. But attending Columbia Bible College was another matter. His father opposed him at first. Gradually, he agreed to allow Gordon to go if that was what he really wanted.

While there, Gordon's life took a new turn. He heard Dr.

Robert McQuilkin. The claims of Christ on every Christian's life came through loud and clear. Besides, Gordon realized, the people who have least chance to hear the gospel are outside America: the Christian workers with the message are mostly right here at home. That did not seem to make sense. Gordon planned right then to give himself to try to even the inequality in obedience to Christ's command. His life was now directed toward missions.

"I never thought about being an architect again," Gordon says. "That idea just faded." He was to take part in another kind of building. So when Kenneth Hood suggested, only half-seriously, that they should introduce the new SFMF movement to other campuses such as Wheaton, Gordon agreed. Their proposal was accepted. They were among the six men to carry the torch. The team travel was a landmark. But it lasted for only a couple of weeks. Would the excitement for missions die down with the creeping anesthesia of routine?

Perhaps—if it were not for the Student Foreign Missions Fellowship. The group met weekly for prayer, confronted each time with new needs in the lost world. Frequently they were challenged by missions speakers. Constantly they encouraged and stimulated one another to keep the goal of missions clear. The SFMF was more than the initial spark. It was its own fuel.

Of course, as far as Gordon was concerned, it helped that the SFMF student secretary organizing all these contacts by letter was not only efficient, but attractive, and just as committed to world evangelization as Gordon. Robbie White was from Greenville, South Carolina, and a member of a vibrant, missions-oriented church there. Soon his future plans expanded to include Robbie, or "Bob White" as she was called. After graduating with a degree in biblical education and some experience in church work, Gordon married Robbie and together they applied to the Latin America Mission.

In 1939 the Housers sailed for Costa Rica. The beauty of the tiny Central American country is impressive. High in the central plateau is the capital city, San José. Here it is "eternal spring" with a temperature of fifty-nine to seventy degrees all year round. The view is of mountain peaks, the blue Pacific and lush green coastline. Rich volcanic soil makes food plentiful. Progressive and relatively stable, Costa Rica was an ideal setting in which to start a career. Gordon and Robbie began evangelism and church planting.

But not for long. In 1942 came the first of many changes that were to punctuate their lives. Gordon's career as trouble-shooter began to form. The Latin America Mission asked them to move to Colombia to establish a Bible institute. In a country where only 15 per cent of the population is literate, any institution of higher education can seem like only a fantasy. But Gordon did the job. There were no academic requirements for entrance. Any Christian young person with a desire to serve the Lord was admitted. To upgrade the educational standards of future students, the church started a day school for children. Not only could Protestant children be taught without the persecution that they confronted in the Catholic schools, but future church leaders would be educated. For six years the Housers gave themselves to that endeavor.

It was through the Christian elementary school that they met Ubaldo. One sunny Colombian morning a policeman escorted the usual group of children across the street to the Escuela Evangelica. Then he lingered a moment, drew Gordon aside and made a strange request.

"I want my little boy to go to your school."

"But that would be quite impossible," Gordon replied. "You see the school year has already started and all the classes are full. Anyway, your son is very young for school." Ubaldo was just five.

But the policeman insisted.

He had shown no interest in the gospel up till then, and the little mission school was started mainly for believers whose children suffered beatings in the regular schools for their evangelical faith. Gordon explained the situation carefully.

"Besides," he added, "the Bible is taught every day here. Every student in the school will be taught evangelical Christian beliefs."

"That's fine," the father persisted. "I've watched the children from school here every day and I like the way they act. My son must learn to be like that. I want him to go to this school too."

After some deliberation, room was made for Ubaldo. The eager five-year-old reported for class bright and early. Surely he won't last long, Gordon thought. Probably drop out after a few days.

But not Ubaldo. He listened. He learned. He excelled. In a few weeks he accepted Christ as his Savior. Now his life was changed so that everyone noticed the difference.

Especially his father. He called Gordon over again one morning. "I don't know what happened to him, but Ubaldo is different since going to your school. We used to have to make him do chores around the house. Now he does them willingly. We used to have to punish him for misbehaving, but now he is good."

But his mother was not so enthusiastic. "Take him out of that Protestant school," she demanded of her husband. Ubaldo knew there was little he could say to make her change her mind. But he would try one more request.

"Mother, come with me, just once, to Sunday school and meet the people—my friends, the teachers, the missionaries. When you meet them you'll see why I like it so much."

"All right," his mother agreed. "I'll come. But that's it. After that you leave the school."

Beaming, he led his mother to the service on Sunday. Monday morning came and the policeman again called Gordon aside. Was this the end of Ubaldo's Christian schooling?

"My wife liked the service yesterday. She wants me to buy her one of those hymn books you use," he said, quietly handing Gordon some money.

A few days later, he was back for a Bible. In a few weeks Ubaldo's mother received Christ for herself! Now there was only the policeman who had not responded personally to Christ. But it was more difficult for him. He was afraid of losing his job if he was even seen at a service. Nevertheless, he was impressed with both Ubaldo and his wife's new joy. One day he agreed to attend a service, if Gordon would meet him and go with him.

Would he really show up? Gordon hurried along to the appointed meeting place. Here came the policeman as planned, but without cap or badge or any sign of official uniform. He had left them in a store nearby. Slipping cautiously down a side street, they entered the church building and sat behind a post. Maybe no one would see him there. After the service, nervous but hungry for more, he promised to come back.

The next week was the same—the unobtrusive meeting, the attempt to hide his presence. The following week, the policeman was at the service alone. No need for an escort. Soon he was standing at the door to welcome others! He too had come to know Christ and didn't care about secrecy any longer.

Before their furlough, the Housers wanted to take a picture of Ubaldo and his parents. "This is for folks in the States who have been praying for you," they explained. "They want to see how their prayers have been answered and know how to pray for others."

"Then you'd better take another picture."

"Why is that?"

"Because two of my sisters-in-law have also accepted Christ." Since then, a grandmother, another sister and a brother have also followed the Savior. In fact, the brother was so impressed with their testimony that he asked that someone go back to his hometown and tell the good news there.

But another change was in store. Robbie became ill. So ill that the Housers now returned to the United States. Gordon was asked to be West Coast representative for the mission. Always one to say yes, he responded willingly. From 1949-1951, they served the mission on the home end. By 1951 Robbie's health was such that they could return. But not to Colombia.

"The climate in Costa Rica is much healthier," the doctor told them. "If you go back to Costa Rica, you can go. Not anywhere else."

So Costa Rica it was. In 1952 Gordon took up church work in San José under a national church. But the need most evident was for Christian literature in Spanish. The Latin America Mission began publishing Spanish tracts, books and Sunday-school literature. And the man to handle this new undertaking? Gordon Houser. From translation to sales, Gordon and Robbie put literature in the hands of Costa Ricans. They opened the first Christian bookstore in the country.

At the same time, a struggling church was having problems. "If we can't solve these things, we'd better close it up," some said. "No," Gordon replied. "Let me have it." From a dying group of twenty, the congregation grew to one hundred twenty in a few years and still flourishes today.

But now another gap was open. The head of the mission's orphanage became ill. Someone had to supervise the sixty children and staff. Would Robbie do it? An experienced children's worker, she was the one for the job. So Robbie faced a new challenge.

"The worst thing about it," she says now, laughing, "was having to bake bread." The girl that had always kept them supplied with bread quit, and there they were—no bread and no baker. "I had a recipe from home that made two loaves. And we needed enough for sixty! Every day!" But Robbie could not afford time to lament: the bread was needed immediately. So bake it she did. She multiplied her recipe, mixed it with a lot of prayer and a good deal of guesswork, and shoved it in the oven. It was a great relief when the loaves turned out well. "I improved as I went along," says Robbie.

There was a greater ministry for her than bread making. One of the children at the home was Betty. "I first saw her when I visited for a fiesta when Betty was three years old," Robbie recalls. "Her mother had died at her birth and her grandfather brought her to the orphanage. She was a delightful toddler then: I remember her singing, 'Joy, joy, joy.' "

But when Mrs. Houser went back to the orphanage as director, Betty was not quite so cute. At age seventeen she was a troublemaker with a bad temper. Robbie watched and prayed for an opportunity with Betty.

"One day she had a terrific tantrum," Robbie remembers. "I asked her to come into my office and talk to me. She stood there in front of me, black eyes flashing defiance. I asked her, 'Do you think the Lord is pleased with this?' "

No answer. Then tears began to roll down Betty's face, and she said, "Everybody thinks I'm a Christian but I'm not."

"Would you like to become one now?" Robbie asked after they talked.

Betty nodded. She became a new girl that day. Her behavior showed it. She took sewing lessons and got a job as a seamstress in San José. Later she went to seminary there and married a pastor. Today they minister to Hispanics in California.

"That's one result when you step into a gap and just do what God opens up for you to do."

But now another gap was opening.

In 1963 the Housers returned home for a brief furlough. While there, they were asked to be mission representatives on the East Coast as well as taking courses. The hospital in Costa Rica where Gordon had been chaplain now needed an administrator. So Gordon enrolled in a course at Georgia State University to prepare him for the task. Another need—another willing response. Gordon went back to Costa Rica to administer a thirty-five-bed hospital.

But this, too, was not the final assignment. In 1964 Gordon and Robbie were asked to work with Latin America Mission's thriving outreach known as Evangelism-in-Depth. Being adviser for this meant that the Housers lived a year and a half in Venezuela and several months in the Dominican Republic overseeing the evangelism program in those countries.

Then the Canadian director of the mission retired. Where would LAM find a replacement? Where indeed but in the Housers? From 1965, Gordon was director of LAM for Canada. It was while they were there they got a letter from Ubaldo's mother. Her husband, the policeman, had died. But the letter was filled with hope. "Thank you for coming to Colombia," it said, "because now we know where my husband is and we know we're going to see him in heaven one day."

"That was reward enough, right there, for the years in Colombia," Robbie says softly.

The Housers lived in Toronto until retirement in 1979.

Though retirement meant a move to Greenville to be near Robbie's father, it did not mean sitting idle. There was still a need for a gap filler. Houser is preaching, helping a small group of believers form a new work in the Presbyterian Church in America.

"I'm just filling in until they call a real pastor," Gordon says, smiling.

His frequently changing roles have caused some to say to Robbie, "What's the matter? Can't your husband hold down a job?"

They laugh about that now, readily admitting that they have had more assignments than most people. "We've always been flexible," they say modestly. "We just want to step in wherever God needs us."

Chapter 12

TO THE AGUARUNAS—
WITH LOVE FROM GOD

*T*he Amazon begins in a tropical rain forest in northern Peru. The smaller rivers that feed it weave in and out of palm-lined valleys, joining the Maranon River, which pushes south to empty into the mighty Amazon.

It is along these jungle river bends that the Aguarunas live.

A large, intelligent but primitive tribe, they had no written language when Millie and a fellow worker went to live among them in 1953. Demon possession, alcoholism, debauchery and witchcraft were very real. Millie Larson set to work to reduce the language to writing and translate the New Testament.

Growing up on a farm in South Dakota, the only sister to four brothers in a loving, Christian home, Millie's world was light-years away from this warring, illiterate tribe. Yet both situations had two things in common. Work and dogged commitment. Millie was well prepared to stick to the task that she encountered.

Over her growing-up years Millie was influenced by missionaries—hearing them speak, having them as guests, reading their biographies. It was natural that, after giving her life to Christ as a child, she would plan to spend her life in missions.

But not until she got to Wheaton did her plans really fall into place. At Wheaton, Millie found SFMF and attended regularly. One day the SFMF speaker was a woman working in Mexico with an agency called Wycliffe Bible Translators.

"By all our best estimates there are at least 1,000 languages yet to go," Velma Pickett said. "At least 1,000 languages with no part of the Scripture translated into them—many not even in a written form. Wycliffe wants to send translators to these language groups, trained and willing to do the job."

Millie saw her direction that day. She signed up then and there to take on one of those untouched languages. "The SFMF broadened my understanding of missions," Millie says, "and focused my attention on Wycliffe Bible Translators (WBT) as the right place for me."

But a bachelor's degree in English was not enough for the job. Wycliffe requires all their prospective translators to attend their training program called the Summer Institute of Linguistics (SIL) at Norman, Oklahoma. Millie recalls, "SIL really turned me on." There she spent the summer delving into linguistic principles; methods of listening to pick up unfamiliar language sounds; ways to record it, learn it, teach those who have spoken it all their life to read it. It even included practice in doing exactly that, working in one of the native American villages nearby.

But there was another phase of training too. Wycliffe requires participation in something called Jungle Camp—basic training in jungle living for all new workers. Surviving this is generally thought to be recommendation indeed. Peru would be nothing compared with the rigid requirements of Jungle Camp!

So Millie began work with her assigned tribe, the Aguarunas of Peru. Sitting at a table on a half-walled verandah, she worked day after day with Nelson, a national helper. With tape recorder, language files, commentaries, lexicons, dictionaries, Bible translations and patience they worked. Study, discuss, compare, study some more, translate, revise, translate again. On and on, year after year, the process was the same. Nelson was invaluable.

"Who was Zechariah's other wife?" Nelson asked one day as they began on Luke.

"What do you mean? He had only one wife," Millie answered.

"Then why does it say, 'Your wife, Elizabeth,' if he had no other one?" Since the name of Zechariah's wife had already been mentioned, Nelson contended, it should not be repeated. To do so would imply that there was another wife as well!

Millie understood and they carried on as Nelson suggested. Time and time again his help was crucial. Only a native speaker can ever really think like a native speaker. To cloak the Bible in Western ideas, even if it was their own language, would give it a foreign flavor. It must be their book, one that they can read easily with clear understanding. To achieve that requires more than translating word for word. It means getting to the real meaning behind the words. What did Luke really mean by this? they asked themselves. Once satisfied that they understood his meaning, Nelson could say it as the Aguaruna say it. Millie was responsible to help Nelson understand the meaning of each passage.

"I will make you fishers of men," for instance, was another problem passage. To compare catching fish to catching men would be disastrous in Aguaruna. To them, fish are not "caught," they are killed. You will kill men? Hardly. Even to say literally "catch men" aside from the fishing metaphor would still be a problem. Catching men means putting them in jail.

"This would make Peter out to be a policeman," Millie says.

Another translator who helped with the final revision was struck by the unity of the message from the beginning of Matthew to the final verses of Revelation.

"It's all just one word," he exclaimed to Millie one day. "Paul, Peter, John, Luke—all wrote about love. I understand what the message is now—it's all about God's love."

God's love was something that the Aguarunas badly needed. Witchcraft had a firm hold on all of them. In spite of Millie's instruction and medical care, witch doctors wielded the ultimate power. Tunchi (the ghost of a dead person) was blamed for most sickness and death. Witch doctors either healed a person of tunchi or told them that that was not the cause and that they should seek medicine. Even Christians continued their dependence on the witch doctor.

Faced with real demon possession all around her, Millie had reason to ask herself, "What am I doing here anyway? I came to give the gospel to these people in Peru, but do I believe it myself?" She realized that she was helpless to do anything about the terrible power of Satan that was all around. What was wrong?

One rainy April evening, Elsa, the sister of Nelson, her translator-helper, was sick. Millie went to see her. She heard her singing the witch doctor's song and talking to demons—at times violent and wild, otherwise quiet. Nelson explained, "She's demon possessed. I wrote a song for singing when we cast out demons."

So while Elsa's husband held her down, Nelson prayed, asking forgiveness for all those present and praying for deliverance for his sister. Then he sang his specially composed song. As Millie tells it, "Suddenly Elsa jumped up. The men grabbed her but this time as she sank back she was limp, her singing stopped and she peered in recognition at those present." She fell into a peaceful sleep, and Nelson declared the demons gone.

Millie saw here the faith of the Aguaruna Christians. They had God's Word and they believed it! God had given them faith to act on his Word and had given them visible results in answer to that faith. She yielded herself in a new way to the Holy Spirit that night. With him in control, she had peace that he was going to give her all that was necessary to glorify himself in that place.

After that, she had reason to prove the power of God over demons more than once. Every time, through the joint prayers of God's people, the demons were driven out. Medicine and education would not defeat the witch doctor, but the power of the Holy Spirit in God's people certainly proved greater than all of Satan's forces. People believed.

The New Testament was finally completed in 1975. Checked and revised repeatedly until it was the best possible translation, it was printed and distributed—10,000 copies in a few short years. Hundreds of believers, churches, pastors, Christian schools, Bible conferences—all flourish today among the Aguaruna because of Millie's faithful work and commitment to God for what he wanted to do in that tribe.

Millie went on from a Peruvian valley to be translation consultant and coordinator for Peru and later academic coordinator of SIL for all Latin America. Today she lives in Dallas and is international translation coordinator of all Wycliffe's work.

It is a mammoth job. But it does not bring any more satisfaction than seeing an Aguaruna Christian grasp a Bible for the first time. God's Word—in their language!

"I never get tired of reading it," one man says. And Millie never gets tired of giving it to still one more group of people.

Chapter 13

READY FOR
TAKEOFF

*L*uke could hear his own heart thumping over the pandemonium of voices, motors, cheers and announcements around him. Luke Boughter was entered in the 1940 National Model Airplane Championships in Chicago. It was the biggest competition that he had ever attempted. After all the weeks of work on the specially designed model, would it really perform now when the crunch came?

His father's unique design allowed the wings to pop off in case of mishap, so they could be retrieved for future use. Powered by a large one-cylinder engine, the three-foot-long plane had a mechanical timer, preset to cut off the power from battery to spark plug in twenty seconds. The competition was judged on how long the plane stayed aloft after that twenty-second power jolt.

Luke's first attempt had been so-so: one minute, fifty seconds. No disgrace, but no prize winner either. This was his second attempt. Nervously he readied the plane on the grass strip. Skillfully he started the engine. Twenty seconds. Power off. Plane gliding. Higher, higher. Two minutes. Three and a half minutes. On and up. Four and one-half minutes. The plane was barely visible. Five minutes. It was out of sight. The timing stopped. He felt his chest tighten. Five minutes! She was still flying up there somewhere.

Luke ran to the road, hoping that a passing car would pick him up and catch up with the plane so that he could get it back. A driver obliged, but it was no use. The plane had gone too far to be seen. He had to fly his back-up plane for the third attempt. The average of the three flights would be judged.

Luke was tense as he stood in the crowd waiting for the announcements. "Luke Boughter from Geneva, New York," the bullhorn blared, "in the Junior-C division. Third place."

He had won a trophy! Third place in the nation! It was a momentous accomplishment for a fifteen-year-old boy. Luke was sure that nothing could ever match that thrill.

Model airplanes—building them and flying them—were the most important things in Luke Boughter's life. Though his parents were Christians and he had been saved at eleven years of age in Pennsylvania, his family had not found a church home since their move to New York State. Though still genuine in their desire to follow Christ, their aviation hobby had gradually taken a lead role in their lives. With his father's help, Luke had a model airplane club for the neighborhood boys, a retail outlet where they could buy their supplies and a busy schedule of weekend competitions.

All that was about to change.

In 1941, the Boughters attended a Bible conference at a nearby lake resort. Their renewed commitment to Christ, and their meeting with other Christian families of like interests gave them a new motivation. Why not see if they could form a church in Geneva? Four families, including the Boughters, bought an abandoned church building, repaired and furnished it; before long, regular services were held there on Sundays. The time and effort required for this project kept Luke busy. When the National Model Airplane Championships rolled around the next year, Luke was not in Chicago. He had found another love.

In the summer of 1942, Luke managed a week off from his job with a navy construction project to attend the summer conference that had blessed his life the year before. It was to be a turning point in his life.

The speaker was Dr. Paul Culley, a former missionary to the Philippines and dean of men at Wheaton. His powerful message challenged Luke. He determined that when the war ended and the country normalized, he would give his life to missions.

Meanwhile there was a war to be won.

The navy needed pilots. Thrilled with the idea of doing what he most enjoyed, Luke enlisted on graduation from high school in 1943. During his days of trying out models in an airfield in his hometown, Boughter had taken an interest in a Piper Cub that was housed there. Touching it, cleaning it, examining it, he gradually built a friendship with the pilot, who allowed him to taxi it along the runway. Hours and hours Boughter had spent in that plane—taxiing it, flying with the pilot, loving every second. Now he would have a chance to really fly—on his own! He gobbled up the training eagerly. Assigned to the V-5 program, he underwent accelerated training at various locations across the nation. Rising to the rank of lieutenant, he soon had a dive bomber under his control.

It was during his time at Norman, Oklahoma, that he met the Navigators. Through a friend, he was introduced to the Bible studies and the memory work plan, as well as the vital spiritual life that the "Navs" nourished. It was training par excellence.

Then one day, on returning from a round of golf, Boughter and a friend heard the news. The atom bomb had been dropped on Japan. It was the beginning of the end. When the war ended, the navy offered a chance to stay in or leave. Luke realized that the time had come for him to do what he had promised. He would train to be a missionary.

So in January of 1946, Luke Boughter entered Houghton College. Not that he stopped flying. Having become interested in an organization called Christian Airmen's Missionary Fellowship (later known as Missionary Aviation Fellowship), he saw the potential for airplanes on the mission field. He wanted to keep up his flying for use in missions. He served in the naval reserve. One day a month he went to Brooklyn's Floyd Bennett Field to keep his flying skills sharpened. This meant that Boughter kept a valid pilot's license all during his college days.

In fact, it was this that gave an unusual dimension to his college career. Five other students at Houghton also wanted to fly. Could he teach them?

Teaching flying would require a plane. Luke and a friend bought a retired army ambulance plane now converted to civilian use—a two-seater Arunca for $850. It would also require a runway. For that, Boughter got permission from the farmer behind the college to use his field. Cutting down two trees, they made a strip that had a 900-foot slope, which required taking off and landing uphill. Nevertheless, the farmer was pleased to have the logs cut, the students had a landing strip and the school was—well, if not overjoyed, at least forebearing.

But there was still a problem to be solved: getting old telephone company wire and scrap wood to make posts. Boughter strung a fence around the field and ran power to it, hoping to keep away the cows. Actually, as he found out later, the electrical jolt was so weak that the sensation tickled rather than terrified, and the cows kept returning to rub against it. Before using the strip, the would-be pilots had to shoo off the bovine occupants, but that deterred neither them nor the cows. The flights continued. Eventually, all five students learned to fly, and some went on to get their licenses.

But another task awaited Boughter at Houghton.

Luke went to college to prepare for service to God overseas. He found few others who shared that goal. The missions prayer group consisted of about thirty people. There was no missions conference and very little knowledge of missions activities other than those of the Wesleyan denomination, though the school had recently opened its doors to a wider clientele and wanted to broaden its interests.

But Boughter's vision was not so limited. From friends in the SFMF groups and in Inter-Varsity at Cornell, he heard about the student missions conference to be held in 1946 in Toronto between Christmas and New Year's Day. Luke went—the only Houghton student. What a week it was! "A life-changing experience," he calls it now.

"I've never before or since seen the Lord speak so intensely to students as at that conference." Luke went back to Houghton College bursting with excitement. He shared this eager new vision at the first chapel service. The enthusiasm spread. A revival began and students, especially men whose wartime experiences had given them a view of the world's need, began to offer themselves for missionary service. They formed a group called "Inasmuch" to send relief packages to ravaged postwar Europe. Along with this grew concern for people's spiritual needs—so much so, that soon an SFMF chapter was formed. It organized into groups interested in specific countries and provided chapel speakers. In no time the SFMF prayer group was larger than the regular school prayer meetings.

By Thanksgiving of 1947, they were geared up for the school's first missions conference. It lasted all week, with missionary speakers in every class and in chapel services. Students and faculty volunteered to help stage this new endeavor, which they called "Missionary Conquest." Growth in missions involvement was spontaneous and dramatic. When the announcement was made in a chapel service that students interested in SFMF were to gather for the group yearbook picture, to everyone's amazement, nearly the entire student body showed up. From a disheartened band of thirty Wesleyans, the SFMF had become nearly three hundred young men and women—alert, informed and ready.

Two years before, Luke had gone alone to the Toronto missions convention and returned with enough lift to carry the whole school. When the next missions convention was held, this one at the University of Illinois, busloads of students were there representing Houghton College. It seemed that SFMF was aloft and climbing fast!

Halfway through his first year, Luke reported to sickbay with a sore throat. But he was not too sick to notice the assistant nurse. The daughter of a preacher, Ruth Payton had graduated from nursing school in Atlanta and went to work in Ann Arbor, Michigan, staying with her uncle and aunt there. In their home she met a visiting IVCF staff worker, who led her to a real knowledge of Christ. The next step was Houghton College for more Bible training. She and Luke met, and their flight plans merged. By Christmas of 1946 they were ready to become engaged.

After graduation from Houghton and graduate school at Columbia Bible College, Luke and Ruth were eager to go overseas. They considered Peru. The newly formed Missionary Aviation Fellowship, with which Luke had been associated, was operating a pontoon plane, dubbed a "duck," in that country. There was a need for nurses. Both Boughters knew Spanish. It would be a natural choice.

But they also knew that the mission they belonged to was The Evangelical Alliance Mission (TEAM). And TEAM did not work in Peru. They did, however, need workers in Portugal. Would they consider it? They did. For twenty-five years they had a significant ministry in that spiritually neglected land.

Besides church planting, there were summer Bible conferences, a bookstore and publishing ministry, and a correspondence and extension seminary program. In a time when no evangelical programming was allowed on Portuguese radio and television, the Christian bookstore was allowed to go on the air with advertisements for their books. This gave opportunities for witness.

But one very significant work echoed what Boughter had done at Houghton—the establishment of student groups on university campuses. With the encouragement of C. Stacey Woods and other IVCF leaders, International Fellowship of Evangelical Students (IFES) groups were formed at Lisbon and other university centers. These aided the Christian students and helped them reach out to others.

Now homeside, the Boughters continue to help the work of God in Portugal and in all of Europe. Working with Bible Christian Union as associate director, Boughter has an aerial view of what God is doing. He sees the targets—towns of one hundred fifty to two hundred thousand with no evangelical witness. And he also knows from experience how SFMF and IVCF in America and IFES in Europe, are helping students get off the ground to accomplish God's mission.

Chapter 14

LEARNING AND LOVING IN HONG KONG

*T*here was never anything else I wanted to be." That's how Bill Commons explains his decision to be a missionary.

Born in Philadelphia to Christian parents, William was influenced from early days by his godly father, who was a minister. "I was tremendously impressed by his inner strength and character," he says. So it was not unnatural that, at age seven, Bill gave his life to Christ after church one Sunday evening. From that day on, God put into his heart "a growing and overpowering desire to be a missionary" that never faded.

It was therefore no surprise to find Bill in SFMF in college. "Missions was the most important thing in my life, so I gravitated naturally to the SFMF," he says now. If SFMF did not introduce Bill to missions, it did stimulate his interest and broaden his knowledge. It made him aware of the opportunities that existed under so many mission agencies. Attending the groups targeting prayer on specific regions of the world was a very real help in sharpening his focus. Bill became president of SFMF at Wheaton during his senior year.

Much of Bill's attention during his years in SFMF in college was directed to a special project. It was a summer missions project called "the Wheaton Twelve." As one of the officers of SFMF, he had a part in organizing and administering that project. Twelve students were sent out in 1958 for the first time. They went to countries in Latin America for a summer of experience. What an experience it was—living with missionaries and seeing firsthand the work, joys, problems and needs confronting them. So effective did that summer enterprise prove to be that it has continued to the present sending out larger numbers of students. Missionaries are in many parts of the world today who gained their first vision and training through weeks spent in one of Wheaton's summer missions projects.

One advantage of being in SFMF was the opportunity to rub shoulders with so many missionaries and get acquainted with a variety of organizations at close range, such as the weekend spent at the headquarters of The Evangelical Alliance Mission (TEAM). The mission invited small groups of ten or twelve students at a time to visit their headquarters in Chicago, meet the directors, attend a prayer meeting and "generally get the pulse of the mission." As president of SFMF, Bill took them up on the invitation and still considers it a highlight of that year.

By the time that Commons had finished college and graduate school, he was well established in his direction to the mission-field. What he was not sure of was the group with which to work. Bill was familiar with the Association of Baptists for World Evangelism because his father was an administrator with that board. The ABWE was founded in 1927 and works today in twenty-two countries around the world. Bill had long respected their policies. But was it the organization for him? Playing on the right team is an important part of winning the game. So Bill read and talked, compared and prayed. By the time that he had completed his seminary training at Grand Rapids Baptist Seminary, he was sure. He too would find his niche in the ranks of ABWE.

Besides schooling, Bill was picking up practical training during these premission years. He served as pastor in two Baptist churches in New York and Michigan. He was gaining something else too. In 1965 William Tracy Commons married Sharon Joy DeJong, a graduate of Grand Rapids Baptist College and a musician. She shared his commitment and goals. That same year, Bill and Sharon were accepted with ABWE and on their way to Hong Kong.

Besides tackling the challenge of Cantonese language study, the Commons were involved in the work of two churches. Before they left for furlough, one of those churches had already become independent of foreign help and called its own Chinese pastor. "These churches have gone on to start other churches, which are in turn starting other churches," Bill says with satisfaction.

Their second term saw the beginnings of an exciting new advance, the Christian Social Service Center. This attempt to meet some of Hong Kong's endless physical and material needs was established in a government housing project. Not only did it reach out to obvious social needs, but, through it, another church was planted and rooted as an indigenous work in three years.

Another similar project occupied Bill and Sharon's third term. Through an evangelistic study center, a second church was formed; in two years, that group too had called its own Chinese pastor. It was during this third term that Bill and Sharon met Lam Chi Ching, Sister Lam.

Sister Lam was a peasant woman. Having few possessions, she and her husband lived in a one-room apartment in a high-rise government-housing unit. She was sixty-five when she came to know Christ. Though illiterate, Sister Lam was an avid soul winner simply by her love for the Lord Jesus and for people whom she brought to him. Every day she reached out from her tiny room to people around her, loving them and inviting them to the services that Bill held in the study center.

"Through her testimony, twenty to thirty other elderly folk were saved." Her joy and peace were remarkable, even in her last weeks of battling with cancer.

"Sister Lam had very little money and almost everything she did receive, she promptly gave back to the Lord. She even persuaded us to hang an offering box in the wall of the Evangelistic Social Service Center . . . since she claimed there should be a place where God's people could give love offerings to him during the week instead of having to wait until Sunday! To our knowledge she is the only one that used that box, and she used it almost daily." Bill counts the impact of her valiant, sacrificial witness and that of others like her as one of the outstanding blessings of his years in Hong Kong. "These outstanding Christians have greatly influenced my life for God. I have learned far more from them than I was ever able to teach them."

With their three children, the Commons returned to the United States in 1980. Bill was appointed director of enlistment and education and is concerned with "educating and motivating congregations and individuals to become involved in world evangelism." He still seeks to encourage SFMF chapters wherever he finds them on the twenty or more campuses that he visits each year. He wants other students to share the joy of missions. Writing for *Classified*, the bulletin that his department puts out to challenge new recruits, Bill says, "Faint-hearted pilgrims who shrink from the challenge of proclaiming Christ to the nations and who avoid strategic life investment for God . . . may never discover the greatest fulfillment awaiting men and women . . . realizing that God actually used YOU."

Chapter 15

"GET UP OR
WE'LL SHOOT!"

Y es, his eyesight can be saved, but it will require surgery and will cost approximately $200," the doctor said, patting the five-year-old's head. "Otherwise I can only promise you blindness."

Mrs. Shedd looked stunned. That $200 was all the money that their missionary family received for a whole year! Hudson had been kicked by a donkey very near his left eye. She had hoped for treatment, but now . . .

"Well, doctor," she said, gathering her courage and looking straight at him. "I don't believe God wants us to go into debt. And since I can't pay you that price, I will have to leave the matter with the Lord. He can heal my son if he wants to."

Calmly, she and Hudson walked out of the office. Blind. Her little boy, blind. Hadn't God given him to her in a very special way? After all, for nine years the doctors had said that they could have no children. And then God had given her Hudson and,

since then, a little girl also. Couldn't God act again in the same
way to prevent blindness from this accident? Yes, she was going
to trust him.

Six months later the doctor confirmed, "I see no evidence of
any eye damage whatsoever. Strange, very unusual," he mur-
mured. Mother smiled slightly. This was just another one of
God's acts of love in answer to her constant prayer. It would be
the same with a wife for Hudson when the time came. She was
already praying for just the right mate for him. God would
provide.

It was with this confidence in the Lord that she and her husband took Hudson down to Cochabamba, Bolivia, when it was
time for school. After a day and a half by truck, they rode another half-day by train. Then in Cochabamba they met up with the
group of missionaries' children and an adult missionary who
accompanied them still further.

"I've rented one for each child, we should be off—take us a
day and a half at least." Each child had his own vehicle—a horse.
One behind the other, the animals with their tiny riders maneu-
vered narrow, tortuous trails up and up, higher and higher into
the Andes Mountains. Finally, after eighteen hours of bouncing
in a saddle, seven-year-old Hudson was at school in San Pedro.

Leaving his parents for nine months of the year was preparation for the big separation from home at age twelve. Hudson,
along with two older boys, returned to the States for high school
in South Carolina. It was six years before he saw his parents
again.

All this, added to the persecution of Protestants that he had
witnessed in Bolivia, made him less than eager to return as a
missionary himself. But gradually the Lord changed his mind. "I
am debtor both to the Greeks, and to the Barbarians," Romans
1:14 reminded him. More and more during his high-school years
Hudson became aware of that debt. He had been privileged to
know the good news of Christ from childhood. Most of the

world's people did not have that advantage. Hudson determined to do his part to balance the record.

At Wheaton College, it was natural for one with his interest to gravitate to SFMF. Here the fellowship with others of like commitment stimulated his desires even further. Looking back, Hudson says that SFMF "set in concrete the urgency of a lost world and what I could do about it with the Lord's help."

It served a practical purpose too—it taught him how to balance not only the spiritual ledger but also a financial one. As treasurer, Shedd picked up skills that were to be used in later years balancing books for missionaries.

There was one more matter of unfinished business before Hudson Shedd was ready for his career in missions. He was not to go alone. Mrs. Shedd's prayers were not wasted. During his second year at Faith Theological Seminary, some friends introduced him to Myra James, a home missionary with the Bible Club movement. She had been working in New York State for three years, hoping to serve eventually in a French-speaking country. She had studied French for four years. Eventually, Myra and Hudson were married, and she redirected her valuable language training to the learning of Spanish. After more than thirty-five years of marriage, Shedd says, "No wonder I couldn't go wrong with the wife the Lord gave me." Mother had been praying.

Together in 1950 they set out for Bolivia under the Andes Evangelical Mission. The five-day adventure to get into their station was warning of what was to come. Conditions were primitive. Education was poor; medical help, scarce. Hudson and Myra found themselves acting as doctor and dentist on occasion because the nearest professional help was over two days' walk away.

Officially, the Shedds' job was church planting and discipling new believers. But a close-up look reveals a variety of ministries. They worked on translation, simplifying the New Testament for undereducated readers, and were in charge of the Bible institute in Cochabamba.

There are other memories of Bolivia, too, some more hair-raising. It was a period of unrest. The government-backed land reforms were causing riots and dissatisfaction. Hudson had been out preaching in the area around Aquile, Bolivia. After the service, a listener offered him a place to sleep—an open courtyard. Wearily, Shedd accepted, stood his bicycle against a wall, spread out two or three goatskins provided by his host for a mattress and settled down to sleep. Suddenly the night came to life. From all sides, Indian warriors emerged, till they surrounded the sleeper. Anger in their eyes, they jabbed guns and knives in his direction and ordered, "Get up and get moving." There was no mistaking the threatening tone. With unexpected calmness, Shedd got up and prepared to walk.

Just then, out of the darkness appeared a stranger.

"Leave him alone," he shouted to the angry attackers. "You touch him and you'll have the whole United States army up here to wipe you out in no time." His word carried weight—the men disappeared as quickly as they had come, back into the night.

"Come on, you can sleep at my house," the benevolent stranger said. If Shedd found himself wondering who this mysterious rescuer was, he did not spend long questioning. With a decent bed and thankful to be alive, he slept.

The next morning he preached again. The previous day's attendance had been fifty. Now, after the incident, the crowd jumped to three hundred. Were his would-be attackers in the group? Hudson could not know. He had not been able to recognize faces in the dark. If they were, they listened quietly. Leaving the results with God, he headed home.

Several months later, another missionary preached in that same area and several made professions of faith. Three of them were among that angry mob that had earlier wanted to kill the missionary. Now they were Christians; their leader was furious. As head of the syndicate, he ordered them arrested and strung up on a cable. Passing Bolivian soldiers saw them and let them go. God was vindicating his own. That same hour, while eating dinner in his own dining room, the syndicate boss who had ordered the attack on Shedd and the arrest of the newly converted gang members fell from his chair, dead.

The persecution of believers ceased. Now free from harassment, the church grew and built its own chapel building in that same area. Today about 100 believers gather weekly to worship God in the very place where they once tried to kill his messenger.

Another problem in Bolivia was transportation, especially the challenge of crossing the many rushing streams. Bridges are very poorly made, and most have given way. For the missionary having to travel, it means making your own road. Thus Hudson was swinging pick and shovel in one remote region to make a road for his jeep to pass. Then his shovel hit something—a railroad trestle! Eureka! Shedd could go across the railway bridge instead of creeping down one side of the gorge and up the other.

But not quite. The ties had long since rotted. The jeep fell through onto the rails. As he struggled to free the wheels, he looked up and saw smoke coming closer. It was the semiweekly train about half a mile away, headed straight for him!

"Please," he urged a man passing by, "help me get my jeep out."

"I'm sorry. I don't know anything about machinery," he answered, pulling away. Frantically, Shedd used a jack and a loose railroad tie. Half an hour later, the jeep was off the track. Relieved, he drove six miles to the railway station and asked to speak to the engineer of the train that he had seen approaching, but it arrived late. "We had some trouble," the engineer explained. "Something wrong with the engine. Couldn't move for an hour! But it seems fine now." Shedd could only mutter, "Thank you, Lord." God had held up a train—just for him.

Besides being a less developed country, Bolivia is mountainous. Living three miles above sea level takes its toll. Hudson developed heart problems, and he and Myra had to consider moving to a lower altitude. So they transferred to Chile to work with another mission, the Gospel Mission of South America (GMSA).

Once again the prime ministry was in Bible training. With four eager beginners Shedd helped in the Bible Institute in Santiago. Later on he became director of the school. Today the student body numbers twenty-five. Always there was evangelism, individual discipling and field council responsibilities.

Then, after eleven years in that country, it came time for another move. Shedd was to be field director in the small country of Uruguay, what Shedd called "the graveyard of missionaries." Though sophisticated and well educated, the people of Uruguay are very hardened and show little interest in anything spiritual. "Very similar to some parts of Europe," Shedd explains, for they seem to have everything but are without God. Only eight-tenths of one per cent claim to be evangelical Christians.

Besides administrative duties, the Shedds used their home for Bible teaching and discipling small groups. There were also opportunities for radio and television ministry.

Of course, in any kind of ministry the real joys and sorrows come from the people to whom you minister. Such was the case with Ms. O. in Chile. While not a full-time student at the Bible institute, she did take several courses. Her zeal was evident in the Bible classes she taught: all over Santiago, she started Bible classes for women and children. She was such a joy. And then one day the truth was told. The Chilean government revealed her identity as a Soviet. She was working hand in glove with the government of Salvador Allende. Not that the political system was her only target. She also had names of pastors and missionaries blacklisted to be wiped out once the Communists took over. She was expelled from the country, never to be allowed back. But such actions leave their mark on a struggling church.

Others, however, were valiant for God. Like Mr. M., a diabetic whose zeal for evangelism drove him to travel everywhere sharing the gospel. But it was difficult to control his diet at the best of times and constant travel made it impossible. Yet he carried on, unceasing, until he died. He was not yet fifty years of age and left a widow and five young children.

In 1979, the Shedds came home, and today Hudson is general director of the GMSA. When not in South America or traveling across the United States, Myra and Hudson are involved in a Spanish-speaking church in Hialeah, Florida, although they presently live in Ft. Lauderdale.

"The doors are open as far as preaching the Word of God in Latin America today," Hudson says. "But I find very few interested in going." So many say they are willing to go but in reality they are preparing to stay. On the other hand, sects of all types thrive across the South American continent, with more growth projected. The incredible inflationary problems that plague most Latin American countries create a realization of desperate need and a search for anything to satisfy. A climate ready for evangelism!

Chapter 16

BALI—PARADISE STILL LOST

*B*ali. *Azure ocean lapping white sand, palm fronds swishing* gently overhead, bronzed bathers sipping refreshment.

Ask Rodger Lewis about Bali and you get a different picture.

Bali is a tropical island just below the equator, part of Indonesia. Volcanic mountain peaks and unspoiled beaches have made it a target of tourists from all over the world. But Bali has remained resistant to the gospel. While the rest of the country is largely Muslim, with strong Christian influence, Bali has remained a Hindu stronghold, with shrines evident everywhere. To Rodger and Lelia, some of the natural beauty fades when seen against the backdrop of deep spiritual darkness. Bali, the tourist agent's dream, is the missionary's challenge.

Not that Rodger was unprepared for challenge. He grew up in New York in a family of five children. His mother had a ministry to the indigent at New York City's hospitals and sang in the Gospel Tabernacle. Her genuine Christian faith held her during the Depression years when her husband died leaving her with five little ones to support. Rodger was seven at the time.

Rodger soon became a problem to his widowed mother—so much so that his grandfather called the police out to the house on one occasion to inspire reform. Stealing from his mother and antagonizing his brothers, Lewis was, in his own words, "a total dirty rat." Then came grace.

At thirteen, Rodger suddenly realized that all the Old Testament sacrifices were just a picture of the ultimate sacrifice Christ had made and that he had made that sacrifice especially for Rodger Lewis, "dirty rat"! He knelt on the floor of the bathroom and accepted Christ on the spot.

The change was instantaneous and total. Being brought up in an evangelical home and a Christian and Missionary Alliance church, Rodger was soon responding to the challenge of worldwide evangelization. "Missions was the highest calling in our C&MA church," he says. "With my gifts in communicating it seemed the right thing for me to do. Besides, it was the least I could do for one who had done so much for me."

So after the army and a year in Nyack College, Rodger enrolled in Wheaton College for a degree in anthropology. He was preparing for a life of service overseas.

That resolve was increased by the Student Foreign Missions Fellowship group he met on campus. Prayer meetings for unreached areas and associations with SFMF leaders like Jim Elliot, Dave Howard, Art Wiens and Ron Weeber made a deep impression on Rodger. "My contact with keen Christians of different denominations was broadening," Lewis says, "and my determination to minister to unreached peoples was strengthened."

In fact, Lewis did more than just attend the SFMF meetings. He was singing in the official male quartet of the college, a position which paid a small fee, when the SFMF president asked him to become song leader for SFMF. He couldn't do both. He opted in favor of SFMF. "I'm glad I did," he says now.

Meeting fellow students of like missionary interest is a big benefit of SFMF. It certainly was so with Rodger. He had actually met Lelia one summer as she worked on the switchboard at Nyack. During his time overseas, letters kept the coals smouldering. Now at Wheaton and active in SFMF together their relationship blazed. Lelia's parents had been missionaries with the Christian and Missionary Alliance, her father martyred in Tibet. Her missions interest and knowledge added to his own. After marriage they applied for service with the C&MA and were assigned to Indonesia in 1953 after three years "learning to scratch and trust God" in a storefront church in Massachusetts.

That's when they found out the truth about Bali.

From 1954 to 1965, the Lewises found themselves in Klungkung, the seat of Bali's Hindu dynasty. There was no Christian witness of any kind. In fact, Rodger and Lelia found themselves butting heads against a "conspiracy of unbelief." Rodger developed a friendship with the former king, a natural advantage for the penetration of the gospel. The old king rented property to the Lewises at a reasonable rate and his esteemed position paved the way for the missionary's message. Even so it took fifteen years to see a church established. To become a Christian was to be a traitor.

Personal visits to village heads, Saturday night films and literature sales on market days brought no visible results. Then a crack appeared in the impenetrable wall of resistance.

Because Klungkung was an educational center, it attracted students from all over the island. Children from Christian families needed a place to stay while there. The Lewises offered them a home. From this grew the Bethel Christian Children's Home which today cares for 153 children—and not only those from Christian families. Hindu children who stay readily believe in that loving environment and go home on vacations to be witnesses to their unbelieving families. Those who graduate and go on to jobs take with them a positive Christian witness to that

"This home is having a telling impact on that still unresponsive area where Balinese Hinduism is a way of life," Rodger says. Today a national church struggles against the current in Klungkung.

In 1966 the Lewises moved to Gianyar. This is the cultural center of Bali, about ten miles from Klungkung and equally unresponsive to the life-changing message of the gospel. Rodger calls it "not so much a church-planting situation, but a plowing-up of rock-hard soil amidst resistant people." After seventeen years there is still no church, but the little group of believers has recently purchased land on which to build. A Roman Catholic priest is the only other missionary of any kind.

Along with personal evangelism, Rodger wrote a Scripture handbook in Balinese called "The Living and True God," did some radio work and carried on a ministry to Indonesian pastors. The C&MA seminary on another island trains an increasing number of Balinese young people. Even more promising is TEE, the Theological Education by Extension program, which makes training available to many struggling pastors and teachers. The Missionary Aviation Fellowship has added its services to this program, transporting teachers and students as necessary. Lelia and Rodger are both "flying professors," teaching advanced students in other parts of Bali and beyond.

The Balinese people have not been the only focus of the Lewises' work.

On the small islands that lie east of the main island of Java live over twenty ethnic groups. The three main ones, the Sumbawans and Bimanese on the Island of Sumbawa and the Sasaks on Lombok Island have over two million people, yet there is still no church among them. Except for two recent booklets in Bimanese, no literature exists in their languages.

"For years we have been the only Protestant missionaries to the Lombok and Sumbawa islands," Rodger says. "Unless Western Christians get more excited about the possibilities of winning resistant peoples, those peoples will remain unresponsive, hidden."

Since 1978 the Indonesian government has forbidden aggressive, direct evangelism. Their plan for Indonesianization has meant adjustments were necessary for all foreign missionaries working there. So Rodger and Lelia moved in 1984 to Denpasar, Bali's capital city, in order to keep a low profile and also be closer to the airport for their frequent visits to neighboring islands. Rodger also holds English-language services in one of Bali's resort hotels.

"It may be that Western missionaries will have to get employment in universities in order to get government permission to live in these areas," Lewis says, referring to smaller islands like Sumbawa and Lombok. But "much help from abroad is still needed for the church is young, poor and inexperienced." Indeed among many groups it is nonexistent.

Neglected and resistant groups will not be won "as long as the Western church is satisfied to sit in the barracks," the Lewises insist. "We challenge the homeland churches to militancy and sacrifice."

For Indonesia's outer islands, it's the only way.

Chapter 17

GOD SENT CHRISTMAS CARDS

T *he year 1947 was a good one. The war over, many G.I.'s* were using G.I. bill funds to complete interrupted education. Europe was struggling to its feet again. The world was recuperating.

Art Wiens, like many others, had returned home after four years in the U.S. Army, serving in Morocco and later in Italy. He had taught school for two years in his home state of Minnesota before the war. Now he was enrolled at Wheaton College to work toward his B.A. He had returned from Europe, but he had not forgotten it.

And God was going to see to it that he never would.

One of the flesh-and-blood reminders that God sent his way was a former army buddy who was now at Wheaton. Henderson had been wounded during his time in Italy and had been in the army hospital where Art Wiens, a chaplain's assistant, had visited him. Now he turned up, alive and well, on campus as president of the Student Foreign Missions Fellowship.

"Come to the Europe prayer group," he urged Art. "It's hard to get people to pray for Europe; they don't think of it as a mission field."

Art knew better. The needs of the Europeans, particularly those in Italy, were vivid to him. He joined the SFMF prayer band eagerly. Knowing the dire physical needs left in the wake of the war, the European prayer band decided to help. They put banks on each table asking students to add one penny at each meal for those in Europe who were hungry. Eventually they collected $1,500 for European relief. Besides that, they worked many Saturdays and evenings putting up "CARE packages" and sending used clothing to needy families whom students knew personally.

But that wasn't all. The spiritual needs were even more staggering than physical ones. Wiens and others who had been there knew very well the spiritual darkness that covered those countries. So they made a special concerted effort of prayer. Daily, weekly, individually and together the students of the European prayer group showered prayer specifically on Italy during that 1946-47 school year. Today in Italy, time after time, when someone tells Wiens how they came to the Lord—often in most unusual ways—it was in 1946 or 1947. God was at work in Italy as students prayed in Illinois.

It was as if God's hand reached from Italy to that Illinois campus and spanned the gap between them in still another way that winter. Wiens had given his life to the Lord for missionary service years before, just two months after he had become a Christian. Influenced since birth by a strong Christian environment in a small town in Minnesota, he finally gained real assurance of salvation one warm June morning in 1939 as he rested the horses out on his father's field. That same summer, at a tent-topped missions conference, a missionary from Ethiopia threw out the challenge of missions and he responded. Missions it was—but where? Did his experience in Italy mean that he should return there? Not necessarily. Yet he knew the unbelievable needs.

His mind was full of these thoughts as Christmas approached. As colored lights twinkled around the town and Christmas trees appeared, Art opened his mail. There were cards from relatives and a letter from home. Then a card from an old friend in Italy.

"Would you come back and work with us when you finish college? We sure do need you."

The next day, another one, and the next—throughout that one season Wiens received seven Christmas cards from the area of Florence, Italy, all with the same request. Seven cards; seven times the repeated plea. Was God saying something to him? The Christmas celebrations around him seemed to blur as he struggled to focus his thoughts. Was this really of God? Throughout January and February of the next year he continued searching.

By spring, he really was convinced God had made his call very clear, and by the time that Wiens left Wheaton to go on to graduate studies at Columbia Bible College his feet were pointed squarely toward Italy.

Along with finding guidance for his own life, Wiens was concerned along with others on campus that other students also obey God's command to go. Besides their already-committed prayer times, a group of them, including Jim Elliot, began to meet every morning for prayer for this very purpose. There were one thousand five hundred students on campus. Why not ask God to send one thousand of them out to the mission field?

So they did. Art began praying for *every* student, going through the school directory. Today Art's tattered prayer diary kept since college days includes five hundred thirty-five missionaries from that period, whom Art still prays for regularly by name! Only well-organized prayer effort of those years can explain the numbers of effective workers around the world today from Wheaton College, class of 1947 and following.

The habit of regular prayer formed in student days was to stay with Wiens as he went to Italy in August 1950. His first year was spent in language study at the university in Florence. Here he met Erma, a Canadian missionary in the same town. In September 1951 they married. At the advice of missions directors, they decided to focus on a university city close to Florence that needed evangelical church workers. Modena, Italy, had one hundred fifty thousand people, and though it had fifty Roman Catholic churches, there was not one Protestant church. It was a perfect target for the Wienses' effort and prayers. They moved to Modena to plant a church. They began simple Bible studies in their home. When meetings in their home were forbidden, they opened a small meeting place. But progress was slow. Many people were interested in hearing the gospel but were afraid to show that interest. Persecution and peer pressure were intense for anyone daring to investigate the evangelical faith. When they opened their first public meeting hall, a priest told people to walk on the other side of the street; even to look inside the Protestant building was sin! Contacts often had to be secret.

But Wiens did not expect instant results. Not discouraged, he continued with meetings. At the same time, they reached out to students through Bible studies and summer camp work. Beginning with one Greek student who was a Christian, student work developed. It was a real milestone when John Carlo, a one-time Marxist, was led to Christ after years of prayerful contact. Today John Carlo heads the board of the Italian IFES movement. He still comes often to Wiens for advice and help, and the student work is very high on Erma and Art's ministry priorities.

Over the years, the Wienses did individual witnessing and counseling, worked on a three-volume Bible commentary and began a radio ministry. Able to speak Italian well, Erma was able to start children's radio programs, which led to the opening of the Italian office of Back to the Bible (Voce Della Biblia) in

1961. Little by little, they saw answers to prayer, such as the eighty-four-year-old Indian merchant, married to an Italian, who heard the gospel on the radio and accepted Christ. Or the four American young people arrested on possession of drugs whom Art visited in prison. Eventually, each of them accepted Jesus as Lord. Slowly the results came, each one precious because of the difficulty. Finally, after nine years, a church was established in Modena. Today there are six such Protestant Christian assemblies and over two hundred evangelical Christians in that city—signs of persistent prayer at work.

God was about to show Art another goal to be reached by prayer, though not in the way that he would have liked. In 1982, Art was hospitalized for tests. Before the ordeal was over, he would spend thirty-six days in the hospital and another six months as an outpatient because of an error made during one of the tests. Wiens lives with damaged lungs today as a result. But the illness was the beginning of a new prayer adventure for him. He realized that the job was too big—they could no longer carry on alone. He began to pray for ten couples to help evangelize the province of Modena. Out of forty-seven municipalities in the province, only six have evangelical churches, though there are individual believers in some of the others. In the past three years Art has seen part of that prayer answered. Four couples have already responded. Now he prays on for six more, praying toward the goal of an established church in each of the forty-seven municipalities. That would be one evangelical witness for every twelve thousand people.

"We also need a full-time couple or more for student work," Art says. The local Inter-Varsity leaders and the Wienses cannot do all that needs to be done.

Six more couples and some student workers. Will God send them? Art believes so. He'll keep on praying. God worked through prayer in college days and in the thirty-five years since. He can do it again. Maybe he will send a few Christmas cards.

Chapter 18

ONE USE FOR
A HEADACHE

*I*t was a headache that got Mary to the mission field. At least that's how it started—or, rather, that was the first that Mary knew of it.

Mary Cooke was at Wheaton College working toward her B.A. Born in Paterson, New Jersey, into a Christian home, she had come to know Christ very early in life. Her mother's godly life influenced her in many ways. Besides, Paterson was the home of the Stams. John Stam and his wife, Betty, were martyred in China in 1934. Mary was seven. The news had spread rapidly among the Christians of Paterson. Maybe that was what led Mr. Cooke to dedicate all his children to God for missionary service.

Perhaps God was using this background to influence her toward Asia, although Mary was not aware of it at the time. In any case, when she went to Wheaton, Mary began studying Chinese with fellow students. She enjoyed the experience, but that did not mean she was going to the mission field.

Then she got a headache.

Unable to study that night, she decided to drop in at SFMF. She could easily slip into the China prayer meeting because the Chinese friends with whom she studied attended it. Why not visit it for once and try to forget about her headache? So Mary went. And kept on going. She never missed a meeting after that. When the challenge was presented, Mary signed the card that SFMF used for those who promised to pray about God's will for them.

"I promised to pray daily to find out if God wanted me to be a foreign missionary," she says. That was the next link in the chain that was to lead to the mission field.

The clincher, though, came in 1947 when Jim Elliot, Art Wiens, and other SFMF leaders organized a round-the-clock prayer vigil to ask God for one thousand students from Wheaton to go as missionaries. For six weeks the vigil continued. Every day, for her allotted fifteen minutes, Mary prayed. Slowly, God led her to see that he would indeed send more students to the mission field. And *she* was to be one of them. "I was called while I was praying for others to go," Mary recalls.

Mary's introduction to missions and her call to go herself began with SFMF. But the organization had a further role in directing Mary. She wanted to go to China. That was certain. But how? The main mission prayed for by the China prayer group was, appropriately, the China Inland Mission, the mission of John and Betty Stam. Mary was convinced that this was the group for her. Following graduation, she taught school for five years, always gaining experience in church and children's work. Finally the big day came. After orientation, she was on her way east, a member of the China Inland Mission, in 1955.

After leaving China in 1949 and 1950, the mission worked in other countries of Southeast Asia. It could, therefore, no longer be called the China Inland Mission. The name was changed to Overseas Missionary Fellowship (OMF), and work spread to nine countries of Asia outside mainland China. Mary was assigned to the large, proud kingdom of Thailand.

Here was a culture unlike anything Mary had ever known. A culture where one's head is sacred, one's feet must not point toward another when sitting, and one's tongue must break the language conspiracy of tones, honorific titles and writing that dares you to crack its code. It is a land where a polite Asian surface covers resistant Buddhist hearts. Here Mary was to work.

Language study was first. Sound by sound, symbol by symbol. Progress came in baby steps. Gradually, Mary learned how to carry on a conversation after the initial head bowing over poised hands and the opening greeting, "Sawat di, kha." Gradually, she learned to follow along in the church service, to read Scripture, to pray, to give a talk. Eventually Mary found herself teaching children's meetings outside under a tree, teaching English and Bible courses in high schools and at the youth center that OMF established. Slowly, but with ever-increasing strides, Mary was becoming a missionary.

Opportunities were plentiful: selling books in schools, evangelism in villages as well as in cities by means of crusades, children's meetings, visitation, teaching English as a means of contacting the upper classes. And, of course, giving out tracts.

It was while distributing tracts that Mary met a dog. A dog that had young puppies, as a matter of fact. Resentful of this foreigner encroaching on her family life, she snapped, giving Mary a serious bite. Mary ended up in the hospital. But God was at work. It was while she was in the hospital that she met the mother of her language teacher. The older lady had terminal cancer, and Mary had the opportunity to witness to her of the salvation that Christ brings. Before she died, the elderly Thai lady had accepted Christ.

All the activity was having results. From the fifth citywide crusade, a church came into being and its people later built their own building. In the rural villages, film evangelism was reaping its fruit too. In village after village, as people watched the gospel at the makeshift open-air theater, their hearts were touched. Some believed, congregations formed, churches were established.

But it had not come easily. Mastering Thai and feeling at home in that land are very real victories. Today, Mary counts as one of her greatest joys "being bilingual and bicultural and the enrichment of such an experience." The thrill of "having Thai . . . with whom to share experiences as close friends" is one of her valued blessings. But it was not without struggle.

Mary has not forgotten those struggles. In 1972, the OMF asked her to assist in the language learning and adjustment of new workers. She supervises the study house where missionaries come for their initial orientation to central Thailand and for a period of language study. Here Mary found that "all the terrible adjustment problems I had as a new missionary became the training I needed to train other new missionaries. God uses everything in your background and training way beyond what you ever dreamed of."

Today, recently returned from furlough, Mary enters another term of passing along what she has learned—that God can use anyone or anything as a tool to accomplish his purpose. That includes headaches!

Chapter 19

PIONEER WITH A PURPOSE

*T*he speaker stepped down from the platform after his message. One person after another shook his hand and asked, "How is Elka?" All over the nation, Christians were asking the same question, "What's the news on Elka?"

Neill Hawkins told them what he could. "We're praying for him," people assured the missionary. Week by week reports came over the radio giving the latest developments in the battle for Elka's soul.

Elka was the witch doctor of the Wai Wai Indians, a primitive tribe in British Guiana. He was the most responsive of his people to the gospel that the Hawkins brothers were teaching. But breaking from the evil spirits was a terrifying prospect. Satan would not easily relinquish this servant of his. The fight was on. Neill Hawkins was in the forefront of that battle. And Christians by the hundreds were waging war. Neill and his wife, Mary, were now on furlough in Texas, and Neill used his father's weekly radio program in Dallas to urge Christians to pray for Elka, the key to penetrating the whole tribe. Finally one day the news came through.

"Elka has accepted Christ." "Father in the Sky," he had prayed, "old Elka wants you to come into the pit of his stomach." Others watched to see if the evil spirits would retaliate. When they saw Elka continue safe and healthy, they too followed his example, one by one. This began a sweeping movement for Christ among the Wai Wai Indians that continues to this day.

But Neill's role in God's fighting force was only beginning. There were new frontiers to be conquered. Neill and Mary left the work in British Guiana with his brother, Bob, and moved back to Brazil, where he was to work for the next three decades. Neill's interest in Brazil really started years earlier.

Pioneering was in his blood. His father was a Methodist circuit-riding preacher and evangelist on the west Texas frontier at the turn of the century. Neill and his brothers were brought up on a blend of Christianity, cattle ranches and camp meetings around their Fort Worth home. Later, when their father left the Methodist church, he pioneered another field—radio evangelism. For thirty-five years, his voice was heard over Dallas radio stations. Neill was used to being in the front of the action.

It was while he was in college that his own pioneering challenge galloped onto the scene—the Indians of Brazil. Three Englishmen, all called "Fred," had been killed trying to take the gospel to the Kayapo Indians. Arthur Tylee, an American, had died a martyr, attempting to reach other Indian tribes. Neill was stirred. Here was a challenge big enough for any pioneer—to bring the gospel of Christ to the Indians of Brazil. This was pioneering with a purpose.

Before that day could come, however, God had another assignment for Neill. It was a two-year lesson in faith that would last a lifetime. Neill Hawkins was made general secretary of the SFMF in 1940 on his graduation from Columbia Bible College.

He traveled from campus to campus promoting SFMF and stir-
ring up interest in missions among Christian students.

This goal was never more clear than at the conferences that
Neill organized in Keswick, New Jersey, right after Christmas
in 1940 and again in 1941. He wanted to give to others the
enthusiasm that pushed his own steps. The world's people are
dying, condemned forever because of their sin. God offers forgiveness and new life, but they do not know this good news. It's
up to us to tell them. It was as simple as that.

Of course, spreading the flame of SFMF all across the United
States meant travel. And travel meant money. Money was one
thing that Neill did not have, so much of his travel was done the
free way—hitchhiking! Neill hitched, not only for his work, but
for personal travel too. One night his fiancée waited for him to
arrive. They had planned a date but Neill did not show up. The
clock hands ticked on. Mary was becoming more and more im-
patient, then angry, then worried. An hour late, an hour and a
half. Finally, two hours late, Neill arrived. He had had trouble
getting a ride. But God supplied during those days, and both
Neill and Mary learned to trust even further the God who was
leading them to Brazil.

Then in 1942 they joined a group that shared their desire for
the Brazilian Indians, the Unevangelized Fields Mission (UFM).
In keeping with Neill's background, UFM was a mission for
pioneers. They pioneered work in places where the gospel had
not yet penetrated. Under UFM, Neill pioneered their first work
among the Makushi and then the exciting breakthrough among
the Wai Wais.

Then it was back to Brazil to plan for a new advance. This time
the target group was the Yanomami Indians of the Uraricoera
Valley. Government permission for that new work was finally
given in 1955, and evangelism among the Yanomami began.
Neill had explored that area repeatedly along with other missionaries and Christian Wai Wai Indians who acted as guides.

It was in the extreme northern tip of Brazil, where it borders Guiana and Venezuela. The gentle savannas of the Uraricoera give rise suddenly to the higher peaks on the Guianan border, which are covered in tropical rain forest. The only way in was by river.

Mile by mile they fought their way upriver, battling rapids. At last they came to the area of the Yanomami. They landed their canoes and went ashore. If missionaries were to work effectively, there must be an airstrip. The people seemed open and receptive.

"Will you work?" Neill asked them. "I have goods to trade for everyone who will do the job." Willing hands appeared by the dozens! Everyone wanted a chance at the tantalizing gifts that the white man spread before them. "Then here's what you must do," Neill explained. If the Missionary Aviation Fellowship could land their little Cessna, it would not only take Neill and his party out more easily but would give a beachhead for establishing a station there in the weeks ahead. No plane could land in the existing jungle. Neill wanted to explain the need. But there was a problem.

Not one of the missionaries visiting the area spoke the local language. Neill would have to use a "video" method. He and the other men took sticks and stood them up on end, simulating trees. Here was a forest. Then they put two sticks together in the shape of a plane and "flew" the model plane over the sticks. Now to land. The model crashed dramatically into the sticks and fell apart. No good. Then they stood trees up again, leaving a small clear space in the middle. This time the innovated model flew neatly into the clearing and landed with dignity. Message received! The trees would be cut.

But there was another problem. Since Neill did not know the Indians' names, how was he going to know who to pay? Furthermore, he was foreman to a crew of laborers who probably didn't have his concept of a workday. One simply worked till you got tired. Keeping accounts was not going to be easy.

Neill made a list of the workers, not by name, but by physical characteristics. Thus the list of employees read: one with a big nose, one with a finger missing, one with jagged scar under his ear and so on. The rest of the problem he tackled by visiting the work site repeatedly all day, every day, noting when "big nose" laid down his axe and when "scarface" picked it up. The payroll problem was lessened if not solved, and the airstrip cleared. Eventually God gave over twenty workers, and the penetration of the Yanomami area began.

Another chapter of pioneering was completed. But Neill Hawkins had new frontiers to conquer. He was becoming increasingly convinced that Brazilians themselves should be taking the gospel to their own country. As field leader for the North Amazon field of UMF, Neill began to recruit Brazilian missionaries for the Indians in the north. It was slow going. But finally, in 1967, the first Brazilian workers joined the Unevangelized Fields Mission. This led shortly afterward to another first, the formation of a Brazilian mission, Missao Evangelica de Amazonia, in which Brazilian and American workers work side by side to evangelize that vast country.

Attempting to recruit potential Brazilian workers was leading Neill to another innovative step. In 1969 he became professor of missions at Word of Life Bible Institute in São Paulo. This is hardly a new post in the eyes of American educators. But Neill developed what he saw was lacking—the first Latin American curriculum offering a major in missions. Now Brazilian Christians had opportunity to get the emphasis and develop the special skills needed to reach out to the Indians of their own land and beyond. Other schools in Brazil copied that plan, modeling their own curricula after the first one by Neill Hawkins.

Of course, the training is lacking if it does not lead to action. Students must not only study evangelism and church planting; they must do it. So Neill took yet another step out ahead. Summer after summer, he led his students back into the primitive

Yanomami area for field experience. This was on-the-job training at its best. More and more of the graduates came back to work there permanently. Eventually 40 per cent of the missionaries in that region were Brazilians, eighteen of them Neill's own students.

Neill's pioneering days were over. In July 1982, he was taken from the frontier of service to a place long prepared and well furnished in heaven for him. Mary continues to serve with UFM, teaching at the Word of Life seminary in São Paulo.

For them both, the commitment made in college was the initial step on a lifelong journey of exploration, claiming new territory for God, blazing new trails for any who will follow.

Chapter 20

AROUND THE WORLD
IN EIGHTY WAYS

*I*f your father is a minister and your grandfather an evangelist, it is not surprising if you become a Christian as a child. That's the way it was with Herbert Anderson. Brought up in a godly home in the Midwest, early on he gave his life to the Lord.

But not until Wheaton College days did he really sense God's claim on him for worldwide evangelization. Under the ministry of L. L. Legters of Wycliffe Bible Translators, he offered his life for missionary service.

Herbert was working his way through school. There was little time for extracurricular activities including SFMF. But occasional attendance at the meetings—along with the influence of a professor, Dr. Jim Graham—wore deeper and deeper impressions on Herb's life.

It was in seminary at Princeton that Anderson really became involved with SFMF. His voice was the link. He sang tenor in the SFMF touring quartet. Peter Stam from Faith Seminary sang bass, Jerry Gerow from Columbia Bible College was the baritone and Jack Armes, also from Faith Seminary, sang second tenor. Together they traversed the southeast, singing and passing along the challenge of students' responsibility to a lost world. All in that quartet have spent their lives in missionary service.

Gradually, Herb's own ties with SFMF and commitment to missions was reinforced. So much so that by 1944 he became the sixth general secretary of Student Foreign Missions Fellowship. This was the beginning of a life involvement in missions. The year and a half spent as secretary for SFMF was significant for him and for the movement. As a result of his tours to Bible colleges and seminaries as well as secular universities, Herb became convinced that a prime source for future missionary recruitment were the Christian groups on secular campuses. Most of these were connected with Inter-Varsity. Could there be some kind of alignment that would benefit both organizations? He approached Stacey Woods, then general secretary of Inter-Varsity, about some kind of cooperation.

"Can we get together? You need the missions emphasis: we need volunteers." It was just after Herb left his position with SFMF that such a merger came about. Today SFMF is indeed an important arm of Inter-Varsity.

Less significant perhaps but just as memorable for Anderson are his experiences while representing SFMF all over the continent. He traveled not only in the United States but also in Canada—even out to the far Northwest, where temperatures remained below zero in early spring. Herb's red, swollen ears burned with frostbite, and he carried the remnants of that "chilling experience" for months. But the response and hospitality at Prairie Bible Institute, Briercrest and the Peace River Bible Institute in Alberta were well worth the frozen ears.

But all that traveling required money. "One incident of God's provision stands out in my mind," Herb says. "I had spoken in chapel and counseled with individual students at the Baptist Bible Seminary of Johnson City, New York. My next stop was Houghton College but I had run out of money. I decided I would not let anyone know my need except the Lord."

As he left the school, Herb remembered a package that he had left behind. He returned to the parlor, picked up the package and was leaving again when a student stopped him. "How do you get money for these trips?" she asked.

"As God provides," replied Anderson.

The girl looked at him and held out her hand. "As you walked back in, the Lord told me to give you this $10," she said.

"It was enough to get me to Houghton and from there on to finish my trip," Anderson remembers.

One other event marked his year and a half as SFMF general secretary. Influenced by the SVM, which preceeded them, the SFMF decided to try a missions convention during Christmas vacation. They chose the National Bible Institute in New York City as the site. How relieved they were when 100 students from SFMF groups around the country attended. "That student missionary conference was a forerunner of Urbana," Herb says.

But missions usually focuses on "the uttermost part" of the world. Anderson did not intend to remain on SFMF home staff forever—he was going overseas. He and his wife, whom he had met at Wheaton College, applied to the Evangelical Free Church, hoping to go to China.

But China was closed. The Evangelical Free board would not take missionaries for that area. Still determined, they applied to the Conservative Baptist Foreign Missions Society. By now Herb was in his second pastorate in Oregon. But he was fully prepared to leave that and go to wherever the Lord led him at any time. To his disappointment, the board's answer came. "We advise you to stay in the pastorate," they told him.

Not go overseas after all? After committing himself for missions, was he going to have to be content with a homeside ministry? Yes, it seemed as if God's answer to his question, "Where will you have me, Lord?" was "Right here." How could he be involved in missions if he stayed in the States?

Yet Anderson has done just that. His zeal for world evangelism has not diminished. Nor has his emphasis on preaching about the Great Commission weakened after forty years. His initial love for God's worldwide work still motivates his ministry. As well as pastoring a series of churches, Anderson has been an instructor in Multnomah School of the Bible, chairman of the Bible and Philosophy Department of Judson Baptist College and later its president. While serving in this capacity, Anderson promoted missions in any way that he could—through chapel speakers, missionary teams, projects, a missions week and organizing missionary prayer groups.

Even more directly missions oriented was the four and a half years during which Anderson served as general director of the Conservative Baptist Foreign Missions Society. As such, he administered the work, recruited new workers and promoted missions in churches across the nation.

When he assumed that directorate, his stated goal was to "see an advance in missionary appointment." "We began a specific program of missionary recruitment," he says. He divided the work geographically among three missionaries on furlough. Each of these, as well as Herb Anderson, visited, spoke, prayed and made every effort to enlarge the missionary ranks. "I began a list of 'my 200' who consented to be on my prayer and contact list as potentials for missionary service," Herb says. "A number of these 200 are now on the mission field."

Even as general director of CBFMS, Herb's experience with SFMF showed through. For missionary recruitment he favors a practice that has been used by SFMF since its beginning—one that was used repeatedly by the early quartet team. He encourages students to sign cards indicating their commitment. There were two cards: A cream-colored one for those who plan to offer themselves for missionary service; a blue one for those who would promise to pray about it. Herb feels strongly about that procedure.

"Many pastors today discourage missionary speakers from making any public appeal," he says. "But most decisions like that are steps in the right direction. Many who are now approaching retirement age after a lifetime of missionary service responded to a public appeal and followed through." He adds, "I know of several who signed those cards who are now retired, having spent a lifetime on some mission field. That's gratifying."

Another emphasis of Anderson's has been missions giving. "How much money was raised, I don't know," he says. "But it must approximate millions." As director of youth ministries for the Conservative Baptists, he was influential in starting a state-wide missions project that doubled each year and is still going on. "The faith-promise plan works," he maintains. "Where this plan has been introduced in churches I served, the missionary giving always increased dramatically!"

Herb Anderson still preaches when he has the opportunity, both here and overseas. His emphasis is still the same. "Although I did not get to the field, the thrust of my life's ministry has been turned in the direction of missions, largely through association with SFMF." In fact, looking back, Herb feels, "the more significant accomplishments of my life have been related to or have sprung out of SFMF."

For Herb, obedience to the Great Commission meant mobilizing more workers, encouraging giving, stimulating prayer— all right here in America. Not exciting? Maybe not to some people. But there's more than one way to have a global impact. For Anderson it is satisfying enough to know that he is doing what God called him to do with results that are felt around the world.

Chapter 21

SING A SONG OF MISSIONS

*J*ack *knew that his turn was coming. The teacher was* commenting on the book report just given. He just knew she was going to call on him next. He had written a report on the biography of John G. Patton, missionary to the Hebrides. What would the class think when they heard it? He prayed, "God, bless this report that I'm going to give so the other kids would listen and might even be interested in knowing more about. . ."

"Jack Armes, if you have yours ready, would you come up and give your report, please?"

As Jack prayed silently and told the story of Patton's adventure with God, he found it not only was well received by the class, but it was a challenge to him as well. God seemed to be asking him for the same kind of commitment that drove Patton. Right then in high school, Jack began to think of missions as his life's work. By the time that he started Hampden-Sydney College, he was sure of it.

Always a singer, Jack joined the college quartet. When he went on to Faith Seminary, music and missions came together. The Student Foreign Missions Fellowship quartet needed a second tenor. Jack was ready! Singing with Jerry Gerow, Herb Anderson and Peter Stam, he spent the summer of 1942 traveling and singing, passing along to others his missionary concern. By the end of that summer, Jack found not only had they lit the fire of missions in others, but a zeal for missions had sung its way even deeper into his own heart.

It was not surprising, then, that Jack would give a summer singing in an evangelical outreach to the Navajo Indians. In cooperation with full-time missionaries to the Indian people, the quartet sang their way west that summer of 1943. They had arrived in Flagstaff, Arizona, for a conference when Jack saw her. Lollie Byram. He was smitten. There was no doubt in his mind from that first encounter that her life was to harmonize with his from then on.

Lollie was born and raised on the mission field—first Korea, then Manchuria. Her parents had stayed on and suffered under the Japanese occupation; finally, they were sent home as refugee American prisoners of war. They looked for another ministry and found it among the Navajo. Lollie, just graduated from Wheaton College, was spending the summer with her parents, so she was at the conference the night that the quartet sang. A nurse and gifted linguist, she was to be an asset to the second tenor with whom she fell in love.

After Jack's graduation from seminary, they were married. They had seen each other only five times. The letters that passed between them must have told enough, however, for there seems to have been no mistake after forty years, during which their duet has swelled to a choir—all of their eight children are involved in world evangelism.

After seminary came a stint as chaplain in the U.S. Navy. Now it was time for Jack to pursue what he knew God had in store for him. Missions. Somewhere.

"We'll go wherever you most need us," they told the Independent Board for Presbyterian Missions.

"Fine. We need you in the office."

"No, that's not what we had in mind," the Armeses replied. "We meant overseas."

But the board was unchanged. "The biggest need at the moment is in the home office." So Armes served as assistant general director for five years. Then again Jack headed toward the mission field. Their offer was the same—"wherever we're most needed." This time they knew where that was.

Kenya. In contrast to the fertile highlands north of Nairobi, where missions were well established, the arid lowlands of the Akamba tribe had no missionary at all. The third largest of forty-plus tribes, the Akamba had few schools, little medicine and almost no contact with outsiders, let alone a gospel witness. They spoke a tonal language, which meant that understanding was determined as much by voice inflection as by letters. "Take, for example, *ngusi*," Jack explains. "Pronounce it with a rising tone and it means 'witness.' Pronounce it with a falling tone, and it means 'a scab.' " Mastering that language was Jack and Lollie's first task.

There were other things to get used to as well—like the music, which uses only a five-note scale. In church services, they often play a type of tambourine made of a wire strung across the tips of a forked stick. Bottle caps are strung on the wire, and the instrument is shaken or tapped in time with the music. As the church grows more mature, missionaries encourage them to make up their own hymns, using native tunes.

The Armeses soon found themselves busy: preaching, teaching, medical work, Bible-school training and, for Lollie, writing and translating Sunday-school materials and Bible-teaching materials for women.

Their chosen area was not a home-owner's paradise. It was low lying and very arid. Crops were scarce. Rains came in November and December and again in April. That's all. Malaria was endemic and serious. The main preoccupation of the people was placating the spirits, whom they held responsible for crops, family, health and every area of life.

"I say 'placating,' not 'worship,' " Jack insists. "Worship implies adoration and love. There is absolutely none of that in the African response to the spirits. It is motivated solely by fear."

Yet, without a doubt, they have been able—from observing nature and using logic—to arrive at some knowledge of God as good, faithful and a God of order. But observation can never give them a knowledge of Christ's saving work.

And that's what Jack Armes had to communicate.

He was constantly alert for ways to do so. In this search, Armes worked on one basic principle: not everything in Western culture is Christian, and not everything in pagan culture is sinful. Surely, there was something in this pagan culture that could be used as a bridge to the people's understanding of the good news.

One day he found it.

Twin boys were brought into the hospital. Both very ill. One of them soon died, and Jack prepared for a Christian burial service. The mother agreed, on one condition.

"You may bury the baby your way if you let me perform our ritual first."

"What is that?" asked Jack, cautiously.

The mother explained, "When a twin is buried, the other twin must die too—not really, but ceremonially. We wrap up the living child and lay him in the grave with the dead twin just for a moment and then take him out."

Armes thought about it and consulted with a national pastor. They agreed there was nothing in Scripture against such a practice and consented to let the mother perform the rite. After the funeral preliminaries, Armes nodded to the mother, who stepped up, laid her living baby in the grave with the dead one for a few seconds and then picked him up again. As she did so, Jack heard her say to the baby, "Now you are a new person. I will give you a new name."

Jack was amazed! Could it be that such a perfect parallel existed? "We are buried with him . . . walk in newness of life . . . if any man be in Christ he is a new creature. . . ." Even the promise of a new name in Revelation 3:12 raced through his mind. Excited, he lost no time using that incident to illustrate to the mother the Christian's new life and identity. Immediately she understood.

Another time, Armes was looking for a way to explain John 3:18, "he that believeth not is condemned already." Born sinners, we are under God's wrath until we come and repent. This was hard to get across. Then he discovered the practice of *kumugua.*

A man whose son has grievously wronged or dishonored him in some way can put a curse on that son. This affects only his own life at first, but if the son does not repent, the effects of the curse will extend to his family and even the whole village. But if the son comes to his father to repent and ask for pardon, he is taken out from under the curse. It no longer affects him or those around him. This is *kumugua*—to come out from under the curse. Now the people to whom he spoke understood exactly humanity's position before God and the need for spiritual *kumugua.*

God was at work among the Akamba in more practical ways too.

The wife of a leper was sent out of her village and told to build her own home. Meanwhile, she became a Christian. When the house was erected she went, but it had no door to keep out hyenas, snakes or errant humans. Fearfully, she moved in, praying for God's protection. When night fell a large German shepherd appeared, parked himself in her doorway and went to sleep. At sunrise, he returned home. The next night, the same thing happened. Every night for a month, the dog slept, curled up in the doorway of that hut, a formidable barrier for any intruder. Meanwhile, the Armeses missed their dog at night but had no idea where he went. Only months later did they learn that he had been sent by God on a nightly mission.

Jack and Lollie are retired now. But the song hasn't ceased. Traveling to conferences and churches in the United States, they still urge others to get their lives in tune with God so that the song of redemption can be sung around the world.

Chapter 22

NO CHILD
OF MINE

*T*he life of an M.K. is enriching ... as we grow in obedience to God," Dr. Bernard Jackson says. He didn't always feel that way. The scene comes back vividly. It was a sultry June day in Vietnam's rainy season. Inside the railroad station vendors padded alongside departing trains, twanging their sales pitch over the huff and push of the engines. Assorted pungent odors and human sounds jumbled unheeded around the little party huddled together on the platform. The moment had come. It was time for Bernard to start school.

Along with his two older brothers and other M.K.'s from the area, he climbed aboard the train to begin the 1,000-mile journey. The Christian and Missionary Alliance (C&MA) school for the children of its missionaries was in Dalat, up in the cooler highlands of South Vietnam. It was healthy, loving and academically excellent—but always, that 1,000 miles stretched between the little six-year-old and his parents.

Hazel and Richmond Jackson were pioneer missionaries on the plains of North Vietnam, known then as French Indochina. Bernard was the third of four sons, and his uncle was the headmaster of the Dalat school when he attended. One furlough, during an evangelistic service in Roxbury, Massachusetts, he prayed to receive Christ as his Savior. But even having the Lord with him did not take away the loneliness of the school situation.

In spite of the lonesome times, the school years passed, and soon Bern was in high school. An even bigger separation now faced him. After long consideration and prayer, Bern and his parents said good-bye and prayed together on a grassy knoll as he left Saigon for high school in the United States. Alone, except for a missionary family who accompanied him, he faced life in a strange land. All that comes back to Jackson's mind when he thinks of M.K.'s. He determined early that he would never do that to any child of his!

After high school he joined the navy. He put his time to good use. By the time that he was discharged, he had gained practical nursing training, operating room technique and medical lab technician training and was pharmacist's mate second class. He even "managed to squeeze in a night course at Honolulu Bible Training School."

At Wheaton College, Bernard majored in zoology and chemistry, graduating with a B.S. in 1952. His background in Southeast Asia led him to others who had an interest in that part of the world—the members of SFMF's Southeast Asia prayer group. Here he found friends; but more than that, his interest in Asia and the needs of the world at large was widened. In spite of the hardships of being an M.K., he had to consider Christ's claim on him for missions. The SFMF kept that claim always before him—sharp, focused, intense. But Bern was headed for dental school, and the C&MA had no place for a dentist in Southeast Asia at that time. Bern kept praying and asking questions as he went on to dental school at Northwestern University.

What *was* God's will for him?

One aspect of God's will was quickly uncovered. On March 7, 1953, Bern accepted a blind date to a fraternity party at the dental school. Her name was Joan Ellen Shaw, a Wheaton College student who was interested in missions—Bible translation, specifically. She was, however, also interested in Bernard. Enough so that after meeting in March they were engaged in May and married in July.

Now they sought God's guidance for their lives together, even if it meant bringing up a family on the mission field. Bernard and Joan had to be willing to obey the Lord's leading. Acting on advice, Bernard contacted the Board of World Missions of the Presbyterian Church in the United States. Yes, they could use a dentist. In fact, the need that they had was exactly one that Bern could fill—a dentist who spoke French. (French was already Bernard's second language because he grew up in a French colony. He also has a nodding acquaintance with German, Latin and Vietnamese.) And since the "C&MA was started by a Presbyterian I didn't find the association difficult," Bern says. But it would be a complete change of geographic focus. Instead of Southeast Asia, which he knew so well, the current need was to teach in a dental school for Africans in Kasai province in the Belgian Congo. "It was only natural to go where needed," says Jackson. So they went. In 1956, on graduation from dental school, Bernard and Joan headed for seminary in Texas and then out to the Congo.

The Congo in the 1950s was a colony of Belgium. From rain forest to cool, dry plateaus, it stretches nearly a million square miles, drained by the great Congo River. With palm oil, cotton, rubber, coffee, copper, gold and diamonds, it was a wealthy, welcoming land. The climate in Kasai province was delightful; there were nine months of rainy season temperatures, "never too hot or too cold," with a daily shower that pelted with deafening roar on the metal roof of their home. Thick mud walls and a concrete floor made their house livable if not enviable.

The Tshiluba language, however, was fascinating to Bern. After studying other languages, he decided that "the structure of this language makes me think it must be one of the most intelligent ones in the world." There were no dentistry terms, or texts, in Tshiluba, though, so Bern's teaching had to be in French. The Institute Medicale Chrétien die Kasai (IMCK) was a nursing and dental school founded by the Presbyterians. The fourteen dental students were given three years of academic studies including anatomy, physiology, pharmacology, hygiene, math, French and laboratory work, followed by a two-year clinical program. Bern taught the dental academic courses; another dentist handled the clinical side. Admittance to the school was limited to those who graduated from the seventh grade and were eighteen to twenty years old. In a country of witchcraft and tribal medicine, the IMCK at Lubondai made a tremendous difference.

While Bern was teaching dentistry, Joan was teaching home economics. As director of a girl's home economics school, she had the credentials necessary to get the school recognized and subsidized by the government. The dental school paid for itself by offering free service to Presbyterian missionaries, half-price dentistry to other Protestant missionaries and full-priced service to the general public. Business and military people—White and Black—took advantage of this. Into this busy and satisfying life were added two children, Peggy and Steven.

But ominous days were looming for the Belgian Congo. The year 1960 was to go down in history as the "Year of Freedom" for seventeen new African nations born that year. Not without pain. Urged on by outside nations, rebel forces began to chafe under the yoke of colonialism. Fanned by bitter tribal violence and economic uncertainty, the fire of rebellion burst into flames. Rebel forces surrounded the Luluabourg airport, cutting power and water lines and shooting wildly. Refugees poured into the

Presbyterian mission station needing protection, food, comfort. For Bernard and Joan, they were days of doing what had to be done with little time to think about their own dangerous situation. Then word came from the embassy in Pretoria, South Africa.

"You have forty-eight hours to be at Luluabourg airport for evacuation."

Joan and the children left first. Carrying one-year-old Steven and leading Peggy, who was not yet two, Joan climbed aboard the tiny Cessna 172 that would take them to Luluabourg. She carried all the belongings she could—her purse and one satchel. Bernard followed a day later with more—the clothes on his back and two suitcases, one of which was filled with disposable diaper liners! As the plane lifted off, Joan knew she was walking off and leaving behind all her wedding presents, her household goods, everything.

"Being a refugee out of Congo . . . meant leaving everything behind," Bern says. "It was really not as difficult as it might seem. Perspectives and values change very abruptly."

When Bern met up with Joan and the children three days later at the Belgian air-force base at Kamina, the loss of things seemed immaterial compared with the relief of being safely united again. From Kamina, a USAF "globemaster" carried them on to the safety of southern Rhodesia. In Salisbury, the refugees were personally greeted by Prime Minister Sir Roy Wolinsky and housed by the gracious Rhodesian people until they finally left for American shores. The nightmare of the Congo bloodbath that led to the birth of Zaire was over for Bernard and Joan.

So, it turned out, was their overseas missionary career. Settled in Austin, Texas, they waited for things to settle down in the Congo, hoping for a return. Finally, in 1961, they resigned and went into private practice. Two more children have joined their family since them, and life in work and church has been very much rooted in Texas.

Was this some mistake? The whole of Bern's life had been missions. Growing up on the mission field, son of missionaries, attending a school for M.K.'s, a member of one of the most mission-minded denominations that exist, his interest spurred on and reinforced by SFMF, Bernard Jackson was "made for missions."

What now? Looking back, Bernard says, "I had resented being an M.K. and didn't want to push it off on anyone else." Going overseas with a family was one of the things that "I rebelliously told my heavenly Father I would not do." Yet he had yielded, and God changed him as a result. "From today's vantage point it seems that my life was planned for my growing." The experiences in Africa were part of that plan. God was making a man whom he could use.

He is using him now. Having struggled through years of evangelism with no response, today Bern is seeing people come to Christ in Texas. In his dental office Bernard quietly presents the "Four Spiritual Laws" as he deals with his patients. Since 1981 over 500 people have responded.

Nor is his early childhood wasted. Words and phrases long forgotten come back as he helps with his church's ministry to Vietnamese. Perhaps this was the field that God was preparing him for all along. Obedience at each step has led to bigger and better things. Who knows what blessing is waiting around the corner?

Chapter 23

WHAT ARE YOU GOING TO DO ABOUT IT?

*T*hey're so tiny that they're not marked on a world atlas. Accessible only by small private canoe, they are called the San Blas Islands, and they lie scattered along Panama's northern coast, lapped by the Caribbean Sea.

The fifty or so inhabited islands of the chain are peopled by the Kuna Indians, who found their way up from Colombia to the Panama Mountains centuries ago. Today, except for a few in Panama City and in Kuna villages along the coast, all live on the tiny coral islands of San Blas.

It was to these neglected spots that Margaret and Claudio Iglesias came in 1949 as newlyweds. They stepped ashore on the islands that were to be their home for the next fifteen years. In the village of Mulatuppu, they started a mission, educated the Kuna children and helped with the translation of the Gospel of Mark. Their three children were born there.

It was not the first time that Margaret had found herself in strange surroundings. Her commitment to God had already led her to step out in faith. Born into a Presbyterian minister's family in Minnesota, Margaret came to know the Lord at a local revival meeting when she was thirteen. She went on to Toccoa Falls Institute in Georgia and Wheaton College, where she earned a B.A. in English.

It was during her college years that Margaret attended SFMF and led the South American prayer group. She met missionaries such as Ruth Stull from Peru and "Uncle Cam" Townsend. She heard messages from great Bible teachers, including Dr. Allen Fleece. And she was impressed.

The SFMF included more than listening. There was also active involvement in outreach. Margaret's choice was teaching the high-school class at San Marcos Mexican Presbyterian Church in Chicago. Though she taught in English, it gave her a chance to hear Spanish as it is used in a worship service. Margaret was minoring in Spanish, but this was the first opportunity to regularly hear sermons and hymns in that language. The missionary speakers and the Christian service that were part of SFMF had a lasting effect on Margaret. She says, "SFMF opened to me a new door on the world and its need for Christ . . . and made me face the question, 'What will you do about it?' "

What Margaret did about it was apply to Wycliffe Bible Translators to spend the summer of 1946 at Camp Wycliffe, a training program in basic linguistics called Summer Institute of Linguistics (SIL) held at Norman, Oklahoma. Here her vague willingness to respond to a general need was brought into focus. There was a need for literacy workers. Margaret had always thought of herself as a teacher, and, indeed, after Wheaton she taught in the Toccoa Falls high school for a year. But here was a specific need in line with her profession, yet more strategic. To obey Christ meant going where he ordered. So Margaret volunteered as a literacy worker under SIL. She was sent to Mexico.

But there was another outcome of SIL's summer training.

Margaret met Claudio Iglesias, a student at Nyack Missionary Training Institute. Claudio was enthusiastic about everything from basketball to evangelism. He had knocked on doors in some of Harlem's worst districts, trying to share the good news of Christ Jesus with other Spanish speakers. His evident love for the Lord and zeal for God's work attracted Margaret. But he was to finish up at Nyack and Margaret was off to Mexico.

There she helped translators to produce reading materials for those who were learning to read. She also helped with reading campaigns in several tribes and came back to Oklahoma to teach phonetics at SIL during the summer.

But in 1949, after two and a half years in Mexico, Margaret was sent home for an extended time for medical reasons. It was that year that she married Claudio Iglesias. Now her mission field would change. Together Margaret and Claudio headed to Panama. That was when the San Blas Islands became their home; the Kuna, their neighbors.

"San Blas culture is very different from that of Panama proper," Margaret says. With no room on the tiny islands for large farms, the people plant corn, plantains or yucca and supplement their diet by fishing and hunting. Their thatch-roofed houses are in two parts—one for cooking, one for sleeping—separated by a small open courtyard. Education is in Spanish, by law, but girls often have no schooling at all, and many children are more at home in the Kuna language.

Lino was one such boy. Walking home one night past Lino's house, Margaret and the boys with her noticed a light. The household was sleeping, all except Lino. There, upstairs in the shadows they saw him, kneeling by a chair with a flickering wick-in-a-tin lamp, struggling to read a new Spanish Bible aloud. Only in first grade, he stumbled along over long names in Spanish— to him a foreign language. Unperturbed by the noises of the group below, he kept right on with his reading till the boys gave up, laughing, and went on home. Today Lino is pastor of a Kuna church in Panama City and heads an evangelistic campaign in a different town each year.

In 1964 the mission field for Margaret changed again. This time it centered in Oklahoma. The Iglesiases worked with the Home Missions Board of the Southern Baptist Church with Native Americans. This time the work was in English. They held Sunday school and church services for students at Chiloco Indian School. In the summer they worked with Fall Creek Assembly Indian Family Camp as chaplain and teachers of children or youth. A special camp attraction, Margaret says, "is singing in different Indian languages with singers who often are in beautiful tribal dress." Indian families have been changed and lives renewed during those camp sessions. During this time, Margaret also wrote a book about the work on the San Blas Islands.

In 1970 the Iglesiases moved again, this time centering in Arizona and New Mexico. Though they continued to help with camp work, their ministry broadened. Claudio bears the title of Catalytic Missionary in Multiethnic Ministries. As such, he is involved in church planting among Korean, Japanese, Romanian, Spanish and Pima Indian groups, right in Arizona. No missionary on a remote field could have opportunity with more ethnic groups than Margaret and Claudio.

Now as Latin America coordinator for CHIEF, the Christian Hope Indian and Eskimo Fellowship, Claudio's outreach is likely to be even greater. Though they currently call Albuquerque home, they spent the summer of 1985 in Panama City helping a Kuna Baptist church with its annual Evangelism-in-Depth campaign. Claudio was invited to return to Panama on a permanent basis to assist developing churches. If they do so, it will simply mean one more change of address. North or south of the border, desert expanse or crowded island, the mission field does not matter. The ministry is the same one that challenged Margaret through SFMF four decades ago—bringing Christ to needy people, wherever they are.

Chapter 24

IT ALL STARTED ONE SUMMER

*T*hey were called the Wheaton Twelve. They were young, eager and dedicated. But mostly they were excited as they stepped off the plane in San José the summer of 1958—excited and a little bit scared. Who knew what might happen in a summer in Costa Rica? This was not your ordinary surfboard-and-tanning-oil vacation. This was a summer missions project sponsored by the Student Foreign Missions Fellowship at Wheaton College. The idea was to give interested students a taste of missions for themselves as well as to be of some help to the missionaries with whom they lived. Forty students applied. Twelve were accepted. One of them was Robert Litteral.

The accepted students were not sent out cold. There was orientation and even minimal language study. For Robert, going to Costa Rica, that meant Spanish. And there was that real-life missionary job of raising funds. The students helped to pay for this experience as much as possible.

Finally they were off. Off to what was to be the turning point in the life of Robert Litteral. He was assigned to work with the Richeys of the Central America Mission. Dick and Jean Richey wanted their young protégé to see as much of the CAM work as possible, so they lost no time breaking him in. The very first weekend after his arrival, Robert was sent to visit Aziel and Marion Jones, Bible translators with the Cherripo Indians.

The needs that Robert saw there were staggering. Both physically and spiritually, this was a needy group of people. What the Joneses were doing was so vital, the Bible so needed, that Robert began to see himself doing something like that too. Throughout the rest of that summer Robert lived with the Richeys, helping where he could, keeping his eyes open. He observed rural work of many varieties with its aching needs and its satisfying accomplishments. This was something that Robert could really sink his teeth into. Was it God's direction for him?

Robert returned to campus enthusiastic about his summer. So did the other eleven. It was, in fact, such a success that the program was to be continued. More students were given the opportunity the next year. Robert wanted to go again. That previous summer was just enough to whet his appetite.

"Can I go again if I cover my own expenses?" he begged. So it was agreed, and Robert attended orientation the second time around. This time, he and three others were assigned to Haiti with Wallace and Eleanor Turnbull of the Haiti Baptist Mission.

This was a different side of mission work. Here the missionaries lived on a central station with a Bible institute. Robert saw the place of institutional missions. He also saw the hurricane relief, food and farming aid, medical ministry, and community development projects that the mission emphasized. Here was a group meeting the needs of the whole person for Christ's sake. Again Robert was impressed. As in Costa Rica, the missionaries themselves were an important part of that impression. Their lives, their willingness to train him, their shared vision—everything left him more sure than ever that he belonged in missions. He became particularly interested in translating the Scriptures so that others could read and understand the message of new life in Christ.

Those SFMF projects shaped Robert's whole future. Although he had gone to college as a chemistry major, he had been convicted that he should be working with people, not test tubes, and had switched to a Bible major. But he had not been sure of his direction until those summer experiences. From then on he knew that his niche was to be Bible translation. The fellowship with others in SFMF and the "challenge of the need and the discipleship required to meet it," capped off by the summer training that the missions project provided, really made the goal clear. Robert Litteral was committed to translation of the Scriptures. He joined the group that specializes in exactly that—Wycliffe Bible Translators.

"The SFMF helped me to want my life to be used of the Lord where the need is the greatest," Robert says in retrospect. "It showed me that my life is to be that of a servant."

After linguistic training and marriage, Robert and his wife, Shirley, were assigned to the Summer Institute of Linguistics (SIL, Wycliffe's name overseas) in Papua New Guinea. The large island east of the Indonesian archipelago and north of Australia is politically divided in two. The western half, called West Irian, is part of Indonesia. The eastern portion, an independent country, is Papua New Guinea.

They were invited to work with the Angor people, a tribe that had no contact with the outside world until eight years before the Litterals arrived. Putting God's Word into these hands was a frightening and weighty task. The first few years of the Litterals' ministry were fraught with setbacks. They had one illness after another, causing them to be away from the village a great deal. And, of course, always there was the language to be heard, broken down, symbolized and learned. Then the written form had to be taught back again to the Angor people so that they could learn to read what they spoke. No wonder that it was several years before the Litterals could communicate much truth about God! Using English, the language of education in Papua New Guinea, and Tok Pisin, a form of pidgin English used by the average New Guinean, Robert and Shirley communicated as they translated. They had cultural barriers to grapple with, however.

The Angor do not speak directly on any subject; they will not say no if they think that the hearer wants to hear yes or if it might mean speaking negatively of someone. Likewise, they will not call adults by their first names, discipline their children or state their business directly. Frustrating indeed to an American! Another cultural characteristic of the Angor is that they do not look at the person to whom they are speaking.

But, with patience and persistence, the Litterals kept at the task.

After a few years, the Litterals noticed a young man named Waf, who liked to hang around their house hoping to learn something. He would stand outside and listen to the missionaries trying to speak his language and put the Book into his words. Gradually he became their language teacher and translation assistant. Slowly they worked together through Genesis, translating story after story. Abraham and Sarah and the promised son, Isaac; Jacob, chosen by God; Joseph, the favorite son who was sold as a slave but ended up a king. Little by little, the truths sank in and Waf gave his life to Christ—the first Christian among the Angor.

When Waf left for work elsewhere, God sent Koiyao to help finish the translation of Mark, and he too became a Christian. Meanwhile, the missionaries were teaching some adults to read. Now Koiyao began to teach reading to the children. After eight years of work, increasing numbers of Christians began to meet together. It was church, Angor-style: everyone sitting on the ground under an extended house roof, leader in front, not facing his audience. As he led the service, everyone felt free to put in his or her comments or questions. Even now, though they meet in a more traditional service with leader facing his audience, they still carefully avoid eye contact with the speaker.

As more Angor came to know Christ, they assumed leadership in educating and evangelizing, some going out to other villages to plant churches there. Three years after their first meetings, they built their own building. Today there are believers in many villages, and there are regular worship services in five.

As a new book of the Bible is translated, the completed print-out is cut and bound into booklets, and the preachers preach from it until another is ready. The New Testament is not yet completed.

From the beginning, the work has all been in the hands of the people. The leadership, the building, the application of Scripture to their culture—all has come from the Angor themselves. Increasingly, they are learning to read the Angor language. Eventually, as contact with the outside world increases and higher education becomes more common, perhaps more Angor will speak Tok Pisin or even English. But until that day comes, if ever ("I don't see all the people in Papua New Guinea speaking English in the next few generations," Robert says), the Litterals have taken God's Word to the Angor in the language that they know best.

As translator, sociologist, teacher and linguistic consultant, Robert Litteral is seeking to make disciples of the Angor. The job will not be completed till a whole people group has the whole gospel. But it all began with one student one summer.

Chapter 25

WHAT ABOUT TODAY?

*A*nd now SFMF is fifty years old, this organization born of vision and prayer. Its past is relatively easy to relate; it is history. What SFMF has meant to individuals, what it has done for the American missionary movement has been, in small measure, told in these pages. But what now?

Is there still a need for SFMF on today's campuses? Does it have anything to say to the student of the 1980s? Will it be around tomorrow? The students themselves seem to think so.

Two students at Azusa Pacific College in California tell of their enthusiasm for their recent short-term summer missions experiences provided by SFMF. "I went to Japan for two months this summer," says Shelby Stearns, "and taught English at Post-ka Christ Church. Little did I know at that time that that was the very beginning of God's process that changed my life. . . . I saw God do things and teach me things I never thought possible. First and foremost God is real!"

Shelby continues, "God taught me that I was never alone. He was with me always! And every time that I was weak, he was strong. Every single time! He would seem to always turn my particular weakness into his strength, always. And that was amazing to see!" She told the student body, "Summer missions is a great opportunity. I advise you to look into it if you have a chance."

Paul Cunningham, the other Azusa Pacific student, went to Ecuador for three weeks last summer. "After three weeks in the jungle fighting off a million insects that thought of repellent as a seasoning, trying to get clean in a murky river that only allowed us to change dirt, and sleeping in mosquito nets that kept out nothing but oxygen . . . it's good to be back!" But Paul adds quickly, "I'm sure I speak for the rest of the group . . . when I say, 'Yeah, I'd do it again.'

"We have been changed. We had the chance to experience a new culture, to help some people to grow closer to God." What other learning situation could offer all that? Paul goes on. "We saw God do some incredible things while we were there. We heard about what he's been doing in the lives of the missionaries there. The seeds of faith were planted by them long ago, and we had the chance to do some watering. To me that was worth it all."

When the opportunity was first presented, Paul says, he wasn't considering anything but a summer of loafing. But finally he committed himself to go and "before I knew it I was headed up river in a dug-out canoe."

Miles later, he says, "We began hauling our bags up the banks of the river to our quarters, a bamboo and wood hut on stilts." Their job—to make an airstrip.

The first day, as he tells it, "with machetes in hand, we trucked through the jungles to the site of the would-be airstrip, and we began hacking down everything in sight. A day and a half later all the trees were cut and ready to be carried off to the side.

We thought a bulldozer was going to come in and . . . make everything nice and level." But here comes a realistic discovery about missionary life—"The tractor broke down and we began grubbing the stumps by hand with axes.

"Eight days later, the entire strip, six hundred meters by fifty meters was cleared down to the dirt."

It wasn't all dirt-grubbing for Paul and the gang of twenty-five. They got an insight into the spirit-controlled culture of the Kiata Indians. The influence of Satan on their lives was "very real. And very frightening!" Paul says.

"At first . . . I became a little judgmental," he admits, "thinking how could these people just let Satan defeat them like that? But, how many different ways does he defeat me? Their sin is no worse than mine."

A less profound but just as practical adventure came "while we were digging the ditches. We became bored. . . . So we began flicking mud on each other. We were launching mud bombs over the banana trees. To the nationals who were watching in amusement, it was a testimony for Christ. You see they knew we were Christians, but they couldn't figure out how we could be doing a tedious task and have a good time and get along with each other. . . . I mean, we're just a bunch of frustrated gringos chucking mud at each other, but God was able to use that to minister to these folks."

Lessons learned through summer missions experiences leave a mark on students' lives forever.

Consider, too, what has been happening in the Southeast Region SFMF (SER SFMF).

With Kent McQuilkin as chairman, the SER council met for daily prayer during the 1981-82 school year. They would pray for a different school in the SER SFMF each day and for any regional activities. Kent (whose grandfather, Robert C. McQuilkin, was instrumental in the founding of SFMF) led by example in praying and trusting God to do extraordinary things.

This concern developed into a regular meeting of the SER council to pray for God's moving. It was this emphasis on prayer that has been the single most important factor in the SER SFMF.

One of the first signs of that development was seen in GO (Global Outreach) Conference attendance. GO is completely organized and run by students. Its purpose is to challenge and inform students concerning their role in the world mission of the church. Following the initiative of students in the SER SFMF other students have organized similar weekend conferences in New England, Chicago, Florida, Washington, D.C., and the Pacific Northwest. GO 83 almost doubled in size as nearly four hundred students attended. GO 84 and GO 85 had nearly seven hundred present.

God has used the GO Conference to direct people all across the southeast into missions. Today there is a young lady teaching English in China as the result of GO 80. There is a young man working by government invitation in a country previously hostile to Christian witness as a result of GO 81.

The emphasis on prayer was continued by McQuilkin's successor, John North, an MK from Australia. John also sought to bring together all the resources of the several different schools into one cooperative unit. This was accomplished to some extent at the Campus Missions workshop—SFMF's spring leadership training weekend held at Columbia Bible College.

Leaders from the SER then began traveling the Pacific Northwest to share the excitement. As a result, sixty-eight students from sixteen campuses in these two regions came in record numbers to the Campus Missions workshops to receive leadership training.

People have been praying all over the southeast for God to do a new work of world evangelism and he is responding. Six new SFMF chapters were started between 1984 and 1986, and SFMF's influence is extending to include secular campuses through Inter-Varsity chapters.

The story of this resurgence in SFMF in the southeast is exemplified in one campus, Southeastern College in Lakeland, Florida. It started on a cold winter night, December 27, 1983.

Up to now, the missions program at Southeastern consisted merely of a few "missions rituals." These included the Fall Mission Convention, bimonthly missions chapels and summer missions trips by five or six selected mission interns. Then Eric Jenkins returned from the Urbana missions convention with a feeling that God was going to do something big in regards to missions at his campus. He began immediately to search for other students who might share his vision for a renewal of missions interest at Southeastern.

Eric found only a few, but those began to pray. For ten weeks they met daily in front of the chapel at noon. Led by Henry Hauser, this group began to ask God for a revival at their school that would touch the world. Then things began to change.

Along with praying, these committed students began to put action to their request. One of them began writing articles for the school newspaper on the need of the world for the gospel. Several of the students began making plans for a Missions Mini-Conference to be held in the spring. This new idea to Southeastern was a success. It was the first time that mission boards outside the Assembly of God denomination had been represented on campus. The impact of the interaction between mission board representatives and the students was tremendous.

Midway through the semester six of the student leaders met with some of the missions faculty members. At that meeting they set some important goals, such as to organize a regional missions conference for college students throughout the southeast and to try any new avenues that might be available to increase the mission vision of the college. Significantly, they decided to organize the movement on campus into a chapter of Student Foreign Missions Fellowship. Within two weeks, the first meeting of the new group, under the name World Christian Fellowship, was held and fourteen students attended.

As the school year came to a close and summer made its arrival, prayers and plans were being made for the next school year. At the forefront of the planning was the Fall Mission Convention whose theme was "Love Enough to Go!" A large tent was set up in the middle of the campus commons and filled with representatives and literature from thirty-five different mission boards. It was inevitable that students would feel the impact. In fact nearly one quarter of the student body filled out decision cards saying that they were willing to go.

The World Christian Fellowship immediately took off. Attendance grew to between forty and fifty. A visitation team visited students in the dorm rooms and discussed the claim of the Great Commission on their lives. The Global Awareness Impact team was trained to visit Sunday schools and teach classes at every level on the subject of missions. The College Visitation Team shared their convictions about missions to Christian groups on other campuses in the area.

Bible studies, concerts of prayer, jungle camp, a missionary training weekend, street witnessing teams and leadership training seminars all prepare students in practical ways for outreach.

Still the growth continues. Over ninety now attend regularly. During the summer of 1985, twenty-eight students were involved in overseas outreach and the goal for the summer of 1986 is one hundred. As recently as February 1986 a regional missions conference on campus drew four hundred to five hundred students from all over the southeastern United States. And there was another sign of mission renewal on campus. The class of 1986 decided to go on a mission project instead of a vacation for their annual senior trip!

This awakening has also had its impact on the lives of graduates. Within a few months after graduation, at least two graduates were already in overseas ministry, and many others were in the process of getting there. Two of these graduates have also founded the Student Mobilization Movement which has a goal of raising one hundred thousand workers for foreign lands.

The story could be repeated on campus after campus. Prairie Bible Institute in Alberta, Canada, has a semiannual biography night spotlighting the lives of missionaries through drama and music. Trinity Evangelical Divinity School finances their summer overseas experience by a four-mile marathon and bake sale at an annual fund-raising picnic. Wheaton's summer project includes youth hostel ministry in which teams of students share their faith with others traveling through Europe. The backbone of the SFMF at Gordon Conwell is a daily, twenty-minute noon prayer meeting, highlighting one country each day.

Moody Bible Institute features monthly concerts of prayer. At Princeton where most students and professors "oppose the group's belief," the SFMF still drew in two hundred sixty Christians from surrounding campuses for a missions conference similar to a small-scale Urbana. Houghton College sponsors voluntary fasts with money going to famine relief, collects pop cans to the tune of $500 or more yearly and, in an even greater innovation, began a "bathroom bonanza." They distribute missions prayer letters and announcements to every bathroom. It's one place that can't be missed!

Columbia Bible College helps to pay for their summer overseas ministry by hiring themselves out as a "servant for a day." Students volunteer to work for local churches and organizations in return for contributions to SFMF summer missions.

This is SFMF today. Pulsing, swelling, bursting with new energy. God is using this gentle explosion to arouse individuals. He wants to use those individuals to touch the world, to complete the last great assignment Christ gave his own.

Bibliography

Commons, William T. *Classified*, vol. 7, no. 3 (Fall 1975). Cherry Hill, N.J.: Association of Baptists for World Evangelism.

Dowdy, Homer E. *Christ's Witchdoctor.* New York: Harper & Bros., 1963.

Houser, Gordon J. "Ubaldo, a South American Boy." New Jersey: Latin America Mission, n.d.

Howard, David M. *The Costly Harvest.* Wheaton, Ill.: Tyndale House, 1975.

Howard, David M. "The Road to Urbana and Beyond." *Evangelical Missions Quarterly,* vol. 21, no. 1 (January 1985), pp. 6-21.

Howard, David M. *Student Power in World Missions.* Second edition. Downers Grove, Ill.: InterVarsity Press, 1979.

Larson, Millie. "The Gift of Faith." *In Other Words,* vol. 4, no. 8 (November 1978).

Larson, Millie. "Greater Is He That Is in You." *Translation* (September/October 1974), pp. 4-6.

Larson, Millie. "What Do These Words Mean?" *In Other Words,* vol. 10, no. 3 (April/May 1984).

Latourette, Kenneth S. *The Great Century.* Vol. 4. *A History of the Expansion of Christianity,* New York: Harper & Bros., 1941.

McQuilkin, Marguerite. *Always in Triumph.* Westwood, N.J.: Fleming H. Revell, 1956.

Mott, John R. *Five Decades and a Forward View.* New York: Harper & Bros., 1939.

"Student Volunteers at Indianapolis." *Missionary Review of the World* (February 1936), p. 68.

"Students and the Modern Missionary Crusade." New York: Student Volunteer Movement, 1906.